Business Case Studies

Renée Huggett

Cambridge University Press
Cambridge
New York Port Chester Melbourne Sydney

Published by the Press Syndicate of the University of Cambridge
The Pitt Building, Trumpington Street, Cambridge CB2 1RP
40 West 20th Street, New York, NY 10011, USA
10 Stamford Road, Oakleigh, Melbourne 3166, Australia

First published 1990

Printed in Great Britain by Scotprint, Musselburgh, Scotland

British Library cataloguing-in-publication data

Huggett, Renee
    Business case studies.
    1. Business enterprise
    I. Title
    338.6

ISBN 0 521 388953

Acknowledgements

**The author and publisher would like to thank the following for
permission to reproduce material.**

p2, 3 Philip Denis Frozen Food Ltd; p5 Association of British
Insurers; p6 Commercial Union Assurance Co. PLC; p8 Social
Trends 19 HMSO; p13 Small Firms Centre, Department of
Employment; p17, 18 Companies House; p24 "Today"; p35
National Westminster Bank PLC; p42 Office of Fair Trading; p43
Capital Radio; p44 Potato Marketing Board; p49 Training Agency;
p55 Department of Employment; p59 Welsh Development Agency;
p71 Financial Times; p79 Fast Frame Franchises; p88 Somerset
Economic Development Unit; p98 Daily Telegraph.
Inside illustrations by Paul Brown

Cover illustration by Oliver Burston.

Contents

'MINI' · CASE · STUDIES

FULL-LENGTH · CASE · STUDIES

F U L L · L E N G T H · C A S E · S T U D I E S

The case studies are all based on fictional persons, firms and organisations.

Introduction

This book contains 50 case studies specially designed for first business courses. There are 35 mini case studies and 15 full-length case studies.

The mini case studies concentrate mainly on a single key topic, such as organisation, market segments, pricing and location of business. They can be used either to exercise newly acquired skills after a topic has been taught in class or for revision. They also provide essential practice for dealing with the component parts of full-length examination case studies and in-course assignments and projects.

In addition to questions, the mini case studies include a variety of other activities, such as report writing, team work and discussion, which help to consolidate knowledge of the topic. Occasionally, they lead students on to other areas of the syllabuses.

The full-length case studies, which deal mainly with the same key concepts as the mini case studies, allow students to apply the basic skills they have acquired to more complex business situations.

Case studies are an ideal way of teaching students on business courses. This activity-based method

- allows students to work by themselves at their own speed, freeing teachers to give individual advice and help

- provides essential practice in applying knowledge and skills to realistic situations

- increases students' confidence in making decisions and solving problems, either as individuals or as members of a team

- reinforces knowledge, and often extends it through the great variety of authentic information provided in many of the case studies.

A Helping Hand

Hilary and Sue had opened their own small restaurant. The restaurant wasn't much to look at, but the meals, cooked by their young chef, Mark, were superb. Unfortunately, not many people were willing to pay the high prices they charged. Their overdraft was mounting month by month, and had almost reached its limit.

A La Carte

Duckling a L'Orange	9½oz	10		
Escalope of Veal a la Creme	7½oz	10		
Breaded Veal Cordon Bleu	6oz	10		
Venison in Red Wine	9oz	10		
Chicken Breast/Leek and Stilton	8oz	10		
Breaded Chicken Breast/Prawns & Lobster	6oz	10	21.90	2.19ptn
Breaded Chicken Breast/Crab & Pink Peppercorns	7oz	10		
Pork Marsala	7½oz	10		
Pork Normande	7½oz	10		
Seafood Provencale	8oz	10		
Plaice Florentine	9oz	10		
Trout with Celery and Walnuts	9oz	10		
Boeuf Stroganoff	7½oz	10		
Boeuf Bourguignon	8oz	10		
Breaded Chicken Kiev	7oz	10		
Supreme of Chicken a la Creme	8½oz	10	17.50	1.75ptn
Breaded Turkey/Asparagus and Ham	6oz	10		
Breaded Veal Escalope	4oz	10		
Lamb Shrewsbury	8oz	10		
Breaded Turkey Cordon Bleu	6oz	10		
Breaded Turkey Waldorf	6oz	10	13.50	1.35ptn
Breaded Chicken/Mushrooms and Cheese	5oz	10		
Breaded Chicken/Pineapple/Cheese and Ham	5oz	10		
Breaded Plaice/Lemon and Garlic Butter	7oz	10		
Chasseur Sauce	2.8oz	30		
Diane Sauce	2.4oz	30	10.50	0.35ptn
Au Poivre Sauce	2.4oz	30		

A La Carte *(Continued)*

Product	Unit of Sale	Unit Price	Approx lb/ptn Cost	
Venison in Red Wine Sauce	9oz	1	2.19	2.19ptn
Salmon En Croute	150g	12	18.60	1.55ptn
Half Honey Roast Duck	10-12oz	10	30.00	3.00ptn
Breaded Chicken Kiev	5½oz	16		
Breaded Chicken/Ham and Asparagus	5½oz	16	15.11	0.94ptn
Breaded Chicken Napoleon	5½oz	16		
Breaded Chicken Calabria	5½oz	16		

Individual Pot Meals

Lasagne Verdi	11oz	12	⎤		**FRIDGEWAY** FAST FAYRE
Cottage Pie	11oz	12		10.08	0.84ptn
Chilli Con Carne	11oz	12	⎦		
Lamb Hot Pot	11oz	12	⎤		
Moussaka	11oz	12			
Chicken Curry with Rice	11oz	12			
Beef Curry with Rice	11oz	12		10.82	0.90ptn
Spaghetti Bolognese	11oz	12			
Vegetable Lasagne	11oz	12			
Vegetable Canelloni	11oz	12			
Meat and Potato Pie	11oz	12			
Beef Stew and Herb Dumplings	11oz	12	⎦		
Fisherman's Pie	11oz	12		11.46	0.96ptn
Potato, Cheese and Leek Pie	11oz	12	⎤		
Beef & Kidney in Ale with Dumplings	11oz	12			
Steak and Kidney Pie	11oz	12		12.00	1.00ptn
Macaroni Cheese	11oz	12			
Chicken and Sweetcorn Lasagne	11oz	12	⎦		
Salmon and Broccoli Pie	11oz	12		12.72	1.06ptn
Cannelloni	11oz	12	⎤		
Seafood Lasagne	11oz	12		14.00	1.17ptn
Game Pie	11oz	12	⎦		
Earthenware Pot with Lid		12		12.40	1.03ea Nett + VAT
Earthenware Platter		6		9.10	1.52ea Nett + VAT

Hilary's Decision

'Something will have to be done,' said Hilary decisively. 'I think Mark will have to go.'

'Oh, no! He's really brilliant.'

'I know; but we're just not getting enough customers to keep us going. Do you know how much Mark costs us?'

'£160 a week,' said Sue.

'And the rest! By the time we've paid his national insurance, and he's taken all the chef's perks, like one steak out of every dozen, he must be costing us nearly £10,000 a year. We just can't afford to keep him anymore.'

'Who's going to do all the cooking?' asked Sue.

'We could buy in all the meals – frozen.'

'Oh, no!' Sue groaned.

Individual Portions

'I've been looking at the prices for individual portions,' said Hilary, handing Sue a list.' Sue studied it.

'They *are* cheap; but why would people want to come here to eat, when they could buy the frozen meals themselves and heat them up at home?'

'That's the whole point, Sue. People don't eat out only for the food. They want something more – a real night out. With what we save on Mark, we could easily provide it. Better furnishings, flowers on every table, soft lights, music, perhaps . . . That would get customers coming in. What do you think, Sue?'

'I don't know. We always said we would only serve fresh food in *our* restaurant . . .'

'But these meals are all prepared and cooked by top-rate chefs. They use them now in all kinds of first-class hotels and restaurants.'

'It just wouldn't be the same, Hilary. If we didn't do our own cooking, there'd be no excitement.'

'Maybe,' said Hilary smiling, 'but that's better than being broke! There's no point in making goods yourself if you can buy them cheaper from other firms. That's what business is all about!'

ACTIVITIES

Questions

1 In your view, should Sue agree to Hilary's suggestion? State your reasons in full.

2 Give examples of any ways in which firms can help other firms in modern business.

Reducing **R**isks

Small Business Advice Files 5

PROTECTING AGAINST THEFT, ARSON AND VANDALISM

INTRODUCTION

Good security is important in protecting your business against thieves and the growing menace of arson attacks and vandalism.

The degree of protection required for different businesses can vary enormously. Protection must match the nature of the crime hazard - the greater the target to thieves and vandals, the greater the security necessary.

No premises can ever be made totally secure, but the objectives of good security are to:

(a) discourage break-ins and criminal damage by the very appearance of the security, and

(b) "buy time" by making it more difficult for intruders to work undetected.

You should consult your insurance company before spending money on security measures. They will advise you of the most appropriate measures available.

Inadequate security can lead to losses out of all proportion to premiums paid. For this reason, insurers often insist on a stated minimum degree of protection before issuing a policy. While such protection enables the insurer to give cover at a realistic premium, it does not normally mean a discount will be given.

KEY CONSIDERATIONS

1. The type of business carried on
2. The attractiveness to thieves of the property at risk
3. The construction of the premises
4. Attendance at the premises
5. Access to the premises
6. The geographical area and location of the premises
7. Security precautions
8. Other security management measures

After working for ten years in various butcher's shops, Mike had decided that it was time to set up on his own. By using his home as a security, he had obtained all the finance he needed to rent a shop and have it fitted out.

He was now considering what insurance he should take out. Like most shopkeepers, he was going to take out a basic insurance package; but he knew that he would have to add on some optional extras.

THE BASIC PACKAGE COVER
automatically included as part of your policy.

It can be arranged in one of two ways:

1. On Standard Basis.

2. 'All Risks' Basis, which means the cover is extended to protect your property and trading profit from loss through accidental damage as well as the other risks.

CONTENTS.

Inflation Protection. Unless you tell us otherwise, this section is Index Linked, to keep the level of your cover in line with the effect of inflation. More details on page 7.

Cover is given for stock in trade, goods in trust, trade and office furniture, fixtures and fittings, utensils, business books and documents for their value as stationery.

Additionally, up to £500 for any pedal cycle, personal effects or tools belonging to directors, employees, customers or visitors.

If you do not own the actual building, you can include the interior decorations, shop front and any landlord's fixtures and fittings for which you are responsible.

All insured against loss or damage caused by fire, lightning, explosion, earthquake, aircraft, riot, civil commotion, strikers, labour disturbances, malicious persons, storm, flood, bursting or overflowing of water tanks, apparatus or pipes, oil leaking from any fixed heating installation, impact by any vehicle, animal or falling trees, breakage or collapse of any aerial, theft involving forcible entry or exit, and hold-up following assault or threat to you and your employees.

If you take 'All Risks' cover, accidental damage is added to the above.

How to work out the amount of cover you need: see page 8.

Special features.

Seasonal stock increases. Most shops increase their normal stock levels at certain times of the year. For this reason, your policy automatically increases the amount insured for stock by 25% during December and January, plus the 31 days before Easter Monday, at no extra cost. If you need more than 25%, or similar cover at other times of the year, this can be arranged.

Trade and office furniture and fixtures and fittings are covered while temporarily removed within Great Britain, Northern Ireland, the Republic of Ireland, Channel Islands and Isle of Man, for up to 15% of the sum insured, though not for theft and hold-up, or storm or flood, while in transit.

Replaced as new. Providing you are insured for full replacement value, we pay the full replacement cost irrespective of age if an item is lost or destroyed.

Computer systems records covered up to £2,500

Repairs and replacement costs to your premises are paid for, if they are your responsibility and caused by damage due to theft involving forcible entry or exit.

Underground service pipes and cables for which you are responsible as a tenant are insured against accidental damage. If you own the building this is dealt with separately under the Buildings section on page 5.

Debris removal costs up to £1,000 are paid, following a claim covered by your policy.

New external door locks and cost of fitting up to £500 in all, paid if keys are stolen.

Principal Exclusions.

Money, securities, coins, stamps, jewellery, watches, furs, precious metals, precious stones or articles composed of any of them or explosives, unless they are specially mentioned in your policy.

If your policy is on a standard basis it does not cover loss or damage to property in the open caused by storm or flood; loss or damage caused by frost; theft from any garden, yard or open space or any building which does not communicate with your main premises; theft by or with the connivance of your employees. Subsidence heave and landslip are also excluded, but can be considered on request.

If your policy is 'All Risks', the accidental damage cover does not include mechanical or electrical breakdown of machinery, loss of or damage to computers and data processing equipment, faulty or defective design, materials or workmanship and wear and tear.

As a way to help keep premium costs down, we ask you to pay the first £50 of each loss.

ACTIVITIES

Questions

1 Describe in your own words the insurance cover that the basic package provides, giving examples of how each item would be important for Mike.

2 What other kind of glass should Mike cover apart from his shop window?

3 Which of the optional extras would you advise Mike to take out. State your reasons.

Letter

Write a letter for Mike to a local insurance broker stating all the insurance required, and asking for a quotation.

Discussion

How can businesses help to protect themselves against theft, arson and vandalism?

Recruiting Labour

SUPERMARKETS plc MEMORANDUM

To: Spyros Demetrios	**Date:** 23 September 1991
From: John Patten	**Reference:** JP/ET
Subject: Labour Recruitment	

Please let me have a report as soon as possible on future policy in recruiting young part-time workers in our stores.

SUPERMARKETS plc

REPORT
Recruitment of Young Part-time Workers

POPULATION CHANGES
According to official forecasts, there will be a great fall in the number of people between the ages of 15 and 29, and a rise in the number of people between the ages of 45 and 59 in the next 10 years. (See attached chart.)

EFFECTS ON RECRUITMENT
At present, we rely heavily on part-time workers between the ages of 16 and 21 for shelf-stacking and check-out work. The change in population structure will reduce this supply of labour.

Educational changes will make it even more difficult to obtain workers of this age group. More people of 16+ will be in full-time education. These students will have much less time to spare, as they will have to work longer hours in both schools and colleges in the future.

GREATER INCENTIVES
If our recruitment of young workers is to be maintained at its present level, they will have to be offered greater incentives. Their pay would have to be increased, or more fringe benefits provided, such as greater discounts, designer uniforms, long-service awards, hairdressing vouchers.

ALTERNATIVE LABOUR SOURCE
However, there is an alternative source of labour in the 45–59 age group, which will be larger than the 15–29 age group by the year 2001, and in the 60+ age group of retired people.
 Older people are more reliable, more efficient, and much more polite than younger workers. They are also far more honest. One recent survey has shown that people between the ages of 11 and 24 are responsible for 56% of thefts in shops and stores, while the over 60s are responsible for only 7%.

CONCLUSION
There are many advantages in recruiting older workers. As this supply of labour is increasing, it would be easier to keep wages and any fringe benefits at lower levels.

RECOMMENDATIONS
It is recommended that:
(a) stores should recruit part-time workers who are 45+ years of age.
(b) younger workers should be phased out and replaced by older workers.

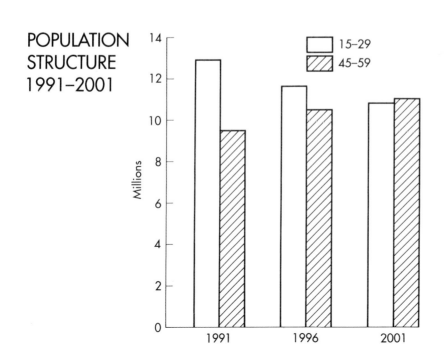

POPULATION STRUCTURE 1991–2001

ACTIVITIES

Questions
1 Why would it be easier to keep wages of old workers at lower levels?
2 In your view does the report give a fair view of the personal qualities of older and younger workers? Give examples.
3 If you were John Patten would you accept Spyros's recommendations, or not?
State your reasons.

Team Work
Design a poster to recruit older workers for display in the supermarkets' windows. (In your team, you will need someone to write the copy, or words; someone to plan the layout and design; someone to draw illustrations; and a team leader.)

Discussion
What other effects are the changes in the population structure likely to have on British business?

Dave and Garry had just been made redundant. They were in their favourite pub, drowning their sorrows in pints of lager, and talking about what they could do in future.

They glanced up as Denis walked in and ordered a double whisky. He peeled off a £5 note from the fat roll of notes in his hip pocket.

'He's doing all right for himself,' said Garry enviously. 'What's he up to now?'

'Denis? Oh, he's got a fruit and veg stall in the market. Just bought himself a new Jaguar.'

'It's all right for some,' said Garry. 'How did he get into that?'

'Through his uncle. He's had a market stall for years.' Dave had a gulp of lager.

'I wouldn't mind having a bash at it myself.'

'Me, too, if it would get me a Jag.'

By the time they met again, Dave had obtained all the information.

'It doesn't cost much,' he told Garry. 'Only £30 a day for a ten-foot stall. Once we've paid for that, we'd be in profit.'

'Say we didn't make £30 . . .?'

'Come off it! Have you ever seen a market trader who was broke? Look at Denis! I've got it all worked out. Garden tools and plants, that's what we could sell. I've found a place where we can get the tools cheap. Make a 100 per cent profit easy. We'd soon be rolling in it.'

'Where are we going to get the plants?'

'We'd have to buy them in at first, but then we could grow them. There wouldn't be much outlay compared with leather jackets or CDs or something like that. If we both put half our redundancy money into it, we'd have a nice little stock to start with. We could get cracking right away.'

'You've got a stall then?' Garry asked.

'Not exactly,' Dave replied. 'You can't just walk in like that.'

'What d'you mean?'

Early Morning Queue

'You've got to be a casual first. Get there first thing in the morning before the other casuals appear, and queue up in case a regular doesn't turn up. Then you get his stall, see. After a bit, if the market super likes your face, he'll find you a regular stall if he can.'

'Let's get it straight,' said Garry. 'You queue up every morning on the chance that a regular's dropped dead or something like that; but if they all turn up, you've had it for the day?'

'That's right.'

'You can keep that,' said Garry. 'I think I'll look for another job.'

ACTIVITIES

Questions

1 Explain in your own words the meaning of the following words and phrases in the case study:

   (a) redundant

   (b) 100 per cent profit

   (c) buy them in

   (d) outlay

   (e) stock.

2 Do you think Garry made a sensible decision? State your reasons.

3 What other enquiries would you advise Dave to make before he decided to set up as a market trader?

Discussion

What personal qualities do self-employed people need if they are to succeed?

11

The Right Choice

C · A · S · E · S · T · U · D · Y · F · I · V · E

BE YOUR OWN BOSS FOR £3,999

YES! for less than £4,000, you could be working for yourself in a booming business.

Owing to an unprecedented increase in demand, we are now seeking more people to take out a franchise for

HOME CHOICE CARPETS

It's such a simple way of making money, we're surprised no one has thought of it before.

We find you all the carpet customers you want. You visit them at home – show them samples – and take their orders. Within days, the carpet of their choice is delivered direct to their door – and you return to fit it.

YES! it's as easy as that. We provide everything you need to ensure that you are earning £££s from Day 1.

● Full training and back-up advice

● Free tool kit containing all the high-quality equipment you'll need – stretchers, knives, measuring tapes etc. etc.

● *National* advertising and *local* business launch.

Like many of our franchisees, you too could soon have a turnover of £100,000.

But that's not all! When you reach a turnover of £150,000, you become a County Franchise Master – with the right to offer franchises of your own throughout the county or city where you operate. So, you'll be making even more £££s.

PHONE TODAY

'I thought I'd let you know that, my first Rolls' – Mr G., Leeds.
Imme

YOUR OWN BUSINESS FOR £10,000

For 10 years, we have been providing fitted carpets in people's own homes. To run a successful franchise for FITTED CARPETS, you need to be physically fit, hard-working, determined to succeed, and willing to work antisocial hours. If you match up to that, you could be earning £10,000 in your first year, and £20,000 or more in year three. No experience is necessary, as we provide everything you need.

▶ Full training by experienced carpet fitters and sales persons

▶ Local advertising throughout the whole franchise period

▶ Management support from headquarters

▶ FITTED CARPETS uniforms

▶ A fully-equipped FITTED CARPETS van, with tools and carpet samples.

Although we supply a comprehensive range of carpets at very competitive prices, you can also buy carpets from other suppliers if you wish. There are now a few franchise vacancies in selected areas at a total cost of £10,000 including VAT. (Up to 33⅓% finance can be arranged for suitable applicants.)

Write, with full details of your career to date, stating why you think you would be a successful franchisee to:

FITTED CARPETS

12

Duncan couldn't believe it at first when he ripped open a letter that Friday morning. It was from a solicitor in Manchester stating that an uncle, whom he had met only once, had left him £10,000.

Pictures of all the things he could buy flashed through his mind: a new car; an extension to the house; a world tour – the holiday of a lifetime. He felt over the moon.

Duncan and his wife Sarah went through all the possibilities while they were celebrating his luck in a restaurant that night.

Working for Himself

It was Sarah who finally persuaded him to take a chance and start working for himself, as he had always wanted to do.

They spent the following morning in the public library, looking up details of franchises. There were a vast number on offer, ranging from car tuning and damp proofing to picture framing. The initial costs ranged from £2,500 to £250,000. Duncan thought he could do best with carpets. There were two franchises on offer – one from HOME CHOICE CARPETS and the other from FITTED CARPETS. They got photocopies of the details and took them home.

ACTIVITIES

Questions

1 What is a franchise?

2 Which franchise would you advise Duncan to choose? Explain all your reasons.

Letter

Write a letter to one of the franchise firms asking for further details.

Discussion

What are the main advantages and disadvantages of a franchise compared with setting up your own business as a sole proprietor?

WHAT TO ASK THE FRANCHISOR

The Small Firms Centre advises people who are thinking of taking out a franchise to ask the franchisor a large number of questions. Some of them are:

▶ How long have you been in franchising?
▶ How many franchised businesses are you running at the moment?
▶ How many business failures have been experienced by your franchisees?
▶ On what basis do you choose your franchisees — how selective are you?
▶ What fees do you charge?
▶ Do you take any commission on supplies of goods or materials to a franchisee?
▶ What advertising and promotional expenditure do you incur?

Finding **A** Partner

Five years ago, Nick Page set up his own business, making hand-made furniture. It was a hard struggle at first; but for the last year he has had so many orders that he cannot cope with them.

Six months ago, Nick obtained an £8,000 bank loan to buy some modern machines. Although the machines helped him to produce more furniture, the number of orders continued to rise, so that he still could not keep up with them.

Nick decided that the only solution was to take on a partner who would be able to share the work and invest some money in the business to pay off part of the bank loan.

He put the following advertisement in the local newspaper.

WORKING PARTNER
required for hand-made
furniture business.
Experience and capital
needed.
Send full details
Box 6249

However, he received only one reply.

Seaview
Waterside Close
Ramford
Westshire

Dear Sir,
I was very interested in your advertisement in the Westshire Gazette for a partner in your furniture business.
For twelve years, I ran my own hand-made furniture business in East Anglia, but I had to give it up. I am now working in a furniture factory in Ambleside, where I have been employed for two years.
I could show you some photographs of the furniture I made when I had my own business, or you are very welcome to inspect the examples I have in my home.
It would be possible for me to invest a small amount of money in your business.
If you are interested, I could come to see you,
Yours faithfully
John Reed

The Meeting

Nick asks John Reed to come to the workshop. John is 20 years older than Nick, but they get on well together from the start.

John's photographs of his furniture show that he is a very skilled worker. He is also full of ideas about new kinds of furniture they could produce.

During their long talk, John reveals why he had to give up working for himself. A solicitor had cheated him out of thousands of pounds profit from his business.

Nick is very keen to have John as a partner. However, when they discuss the terms of the partnership, they run into problems.

John says he is willing to invest £3,000; but he wants 50 per cent of the profits because he has had much more experience. John also says that he is not very keen to have a deed of partnership drawn up by a solicitor, because of his bad experience with the solicitor in the past.

ACTIVITIES

Questions
1   What are the main advantages and disadvantages of partnerships?

2   Why is it necessary to have a written agreement?

3   What are the three most important points that should be included in a partnership agreement? Give your reasons.

4   What actions would you advise Nick to take?

Role Play
Find a partner. One person takes the role of Nick; the other the role of John. Nick should try to persuade John to change his conditions for the partnership.

B*elt* U*p!*

Eighteen months ago, two young sisters opened a small shop selling belts of all kinds for men and women – fashion accessory and trouser belts, money belts, key belts, and sports belts.

Karen and Julia spent a long time choosing the name for their shop. They were both very pleased with the name they chose – Belt Up! – as it seemed to attract just the right kind of customer.

E*xpansion* P*lans*

Their business partnership has done so well that they have decided to expand. They plan to move to a much bigger shop in the high street, and open two other branches elsewhere. After that, they want to print a direct-mail catalogue which will be sent to targeted consumers through a mailing-list service.

They have worked out all the details of their expansion plans. All they need now is the money to finance it – £300,000.

They have already asked their bank manager for a loan. He would only lend them enough money to open the high-street shop, because he thought they were trying to expand their business too fast.

However, a number of people whom they have met through their business have been far more enthusiastic. Some of them have already said they might be interested in investing in the business – if it became a limited company.

Limited Company

'There's nothing else for it,' said Karen. 'We'll have to form a company if we want to raise the money.'

'Oh, I wouldn't like that at all. We haven't got enough money to buy 51 per cent of the shares. We'd be minority shareholders.'

'That's right, but we'd still be running the business from day to day.'

'It wouldn't be the same, Karen. If we had outsiders in the business, we'd never know what they might want to do.'

'They wouldn't interfere as long as we were making good profits. In any case, Julia, if we remain a partnership, we're personally responsible for all the debts if anything does go wrong.'

'That's never bothered us up to now.'

Valuable Asset

'It might do if we expand. There's another thing, too. At the moment, anyone can open a shop and call it "Belt Up!". Once it's registered as a company name, no one else can use it. Our name is too valuable an asset to lose.'

'Oh, I don't know,' said Julia, who was always far more cautious than her older sister. 'Maybe the bank manager was right after all. Perhaps we *are* trying to expand too fast. What if we formed a company and just opened the high-street shop? We could raise enough money then to buy the majority of the shares, so we'd still be in full control.'

ACTIVITIES

Questions

1 Explain the meaning of the following phrases in the case study:

(a) direct mail

(b) targeted consumers

(c) limited company

(d) minority shareholders

(e) valuable asset

2 What are the main advantages of a limited company compared with a partnership?

3 What would you advise the sisters to do about their expansion plans? Explain your reasons in full.

1. INTRODUCTION

When choosing a company name, it is particularly important that persons forming companies should satisfy themselves in advance on the acceptability of the proposed name, bearing in mind that an objection might be received which could result in the company being directed to change its name.

2. Broadly a company name will not be registered if:

(a) it is the same as a name already appearing on the Index of Company names maintained by the Registrar of Companies;

(b) it contains the words 'Limited', 'Unlimited' or 'Public Limited Company', or their Welsh equivalents, or abbreviations of these words except at the end of the name;

(c) in the opinion of the Secretary of State it is offensive;

(d) in the opinion of the Secretary of State its use would constitute a criminal offence.

3. HOW TO REGISTER A COMPANY NAME

Applicants are advised to check whether the name proposed is the same as one already registered by reference to the Index which can be inspected free of charge in the Public Search Rooms at Cardiff, Edinburgh and London. In determining whether one name is 'the same as' another, certain words and their abbreviations, together with accents and punctuation marks, will be disregarded. These words include the definite article and the words 'company', 'limited', 'public limited company' etc. and their Welsh equivalents, whilst 'and' and '&' will be taken to be the same. Names which are phonetically identical but not visually identical will be allowed as not being 'the same as'.

4. If the name is not the same as one already on the Index, and does not require the prior approval of the Secretary of State, the incorporation documents or, in the case of a change of name, the necessary special resolution, should be submitted to the appropriate Registrar of Companies. If the name is acceptable within the provisions of the Act described in these Notes and the documents are correctly completed, the company name will then be registered and the certificate of incorporation issued.

5. For all names which require the approval of the Secretary of State, applicants should seek the advice of Companies House, either in Cardiff for companies intending to have their registered office in England or Wales, or in Edinburgh for companies intending to have their registered office in Scotland. Details about the requirements on the use of the name will then be sent to the applicant.

If the name includes any of the words or expressions listed in Appendix A further information will probably be required to support the application and the applicant will be advised accordingly. If the name contains any of the words or expressions listed in Appendix B applicants will be required to request the relevant body in writing to indicate whether (and if so, why) it has any objections to the proposal to use the word or expression in the name. A statement that such a request has been made, together with any response received from the relevant body, together with the appropriate registration documents, should then be submitted to Companies House.

6. The use of certain words and expressions in company names is covered by other legislation and their improper use may constitute a criminal offence. Those known to the Department are shown at Appendix C, together with details of the relevant legislation and the name of the body which may be asked to provide evidence that the legislation in question is not being contravened. Applicants should initially seek the advice of the appropriate Companies House about any names which contain these words and expressions.

Source: Extracts from 'Company Names: Notes for Guidance', Companies House.

Sale of Council Assets

COUNCIL SELLS PARK TO LONDON PROPERTY DEVELOPER
Protests from Public Gallery

There were hisses and boos from the packed public gallery at a meeting of Eastshire District Council on Tuesday, when it was announced that Eastshire's Victoria Park was to be sold to a London property developer.

The uproar was so great that the meeting had to be suspended for police to clear the public gallery.

The announcement was made by Mr John Priory, chairman of the Parks and Recreation Committee. Despite repeated questions from the Labour opposition, he refused to state the price, as the council was still involved in final negotiations with the firm – Better Developments plc. He revealed that it was a six-figure sum.

Mr Priory said that the deal would be of great benefit to Eastshire. It would provide much-needed cash, and save the expense of running the park. This would allow the council to provide better public services, particularly for senior citizens.

The Editor
Eastshire Gazette
Dear Sir
I should like to reply to some of the wilder charges made by the Labour opposition at the last Council meeting about the sale of Victoria Park to this company.

As residents of Eastshire know, the Council has been unable to maintain the park to the previous high standards. This company intends to plant many new trees and flower beds and ensure that the grass is cut regularly.

New amenities will be provided. In Stage 1 of the development, there will be new tennis courts and a skateboarding park.

It is totally false to say that the new houses in the park will be built only for rich outsiders. In fact, there will be a variety of homes, including some starter units and retirement homes.

All of these developments will bring many new jobs to the area.
Yours faithfully
Ronald Smith
Public Liaison Officer
Better Developments plc

The Editor
Eastshire Gazette
Dear Sir
It is really wicked of the Council to sell off our beautiful Victoria Park.

I have been using the park for 60 years now, and I know it will never be the same again.

We old people do not want noisy skateboarding parks, but peace and quiet.

Neither do we want an estate of new houses spoiling our lovely views.
Yours faithfully
DISGUSTED
(Name and address supplied)

Forecast Annual Savings on Victoria Park

Expenditure	(£)	Income	(£)
Maintenance	41,723	Rent of café	2,750
Plants etc	17,201	Sale of plants	725
Administration	6,128		3,475
Café repairs	2,916	Balance	64,493
	67,968		67,968

ACTIVITIES

Questions

1 Describe what Better Developments plc plan to do with Victoria Park.

2 What would the council gain from selling the park?

3 Who would gain most, and who would lose most, from the sale of the park — the developers, the council, or the members of the public?

4 In your view, should the council have sold the park? Explain your reasons.

Discussion

Has the sale of national and council assets been of benefit or not to the whole community?

Finding A Shop

Karawan is looking for premises for a launderette. Dave, the commercial manager in a local estate agent's, is taking her to look at two shops.

They visit Wellington Road first.

'As you can see,' said Dave, 'the premises are in really first-rate condition. They've been very well maintained. I must say there's a great deal of interest in the shop. In fact, just after you rang, two other people phoned about it.'

'What was it used for previously?'

'It was a boutique.'

'Would I have to get permission for change of use?'

Dave consulted some papers. 'No, there'd be no problem about that.'

'I see the next rent review is in two years' time,' said Karawan. 'Have you any idea what the new rent will be?'

'It's far too early to say yet,' said Dave. 'The commercial market is a little fluid at the moment. But, the owners have always been pretty reasonable with their rent increases.'

'There's one thing that bothers me,' said Karawan. 'I notice there are double lines outside the shop.'

'That's no problem. There's a car park just off Stiles Road. In any case most people walk to launderettes, don't they?'

WELLINGTON ROAD

Annual Rent	£7000
Business Rates	£2000
	£9000

Victorian houses converted to bed sitters

CAR PARK

VINCENT ROAD

STILES ROAD

BUS STOP

• BUS STOP

Residential YMCA

WELLINGTON ROAD

SHOP

HIGH STREET

Police Station

COUNCIL FLATS

SHEPHERDS HILL

NEW LANE

BUS DEPOT

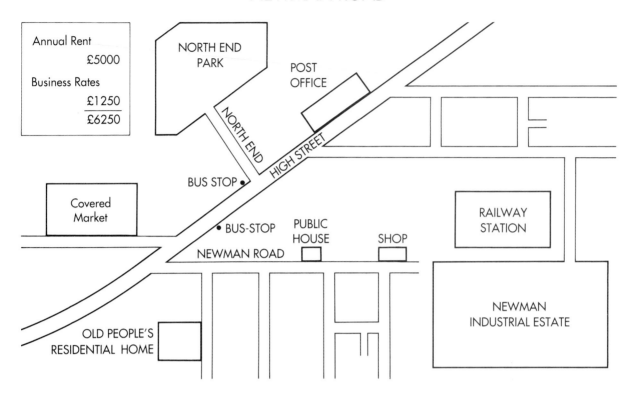

Real Bargain

They then went on to Newman Road.

'This is a real bargain,' said Dave. 'It's a very low rent for a shop just off the high street and the next rent review is five years away. It could be just what you're looking for. As you can see, it was used as a launderette before. The plumbing's all in place, so you've only got to hire the machines and you're in business.'

'What happened to the previous owner?'

'I'm not quite sure. My assistant handled these premises. I think the owner retired,' Dave added, rather vaguely. 'He must have done quite well anyway. There are lots of young families in flats around here. They must have been pleased to have a launderette so handy. And there's no problem with parking. There are no yellow lines in the little streets off Newman Road.'

ACTIVITIES

Questions
1 What is meant in business by 'change of use'?

2 Who gives permission for a change of use?

3 Which shop seems to be most suitable for Karawan's business? State your reasons.

4 What further information should Karawan obtain before she comes to a firm decision?

New Management Structure

A firm which exports 60 per cent of its products to other European Community countries is changing its management structure to meet the increased competition in 1992. Its present structure is:

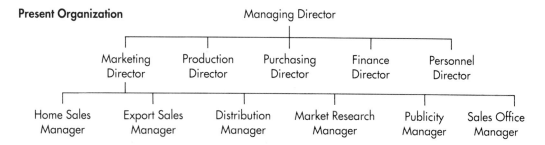

Present Organization

Managing Director

Marketing Director — Production Director — Purchasing Director — Finance Director — Personnel Director

Home Sales Manager — Export Sales Manager — Distribution Manager — Market Research Manager — Publicity Manager — Sales Office Manager

Top management has proposed the changes shown in the chart below:

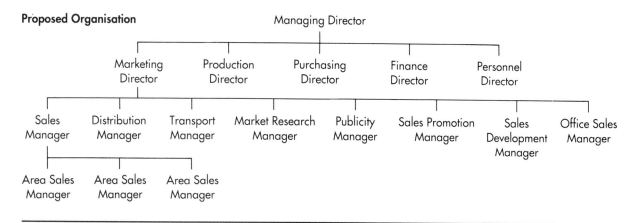

Proposed Organisation

Managing Director

Marketing Director — Production Director — Purchasing Director — Finance Director — Personnel Director

Sales Manager — Distribution Manager — Transport Manager — Market Research Manager — Publicity Manager — Sales Promotion Manager — Sales Development Manager — Office Sales Manager

Area Sales Manager — Area Sales Manager — Area Sales Manager

ACTIVITIES

Questions

1 What new posts would be created by the proposed change in structure?

2 What will be the effects of the proposed changes on the Marketing Director's span of control?

3 In your view, why is it planned to have only one Sales Manager instead of two?

Report

Write a report stating whether you would recommend the proposed structure.

Discussion

What will be the advantages and disadvantages of 1992 for British business?

Days Out

C A S E · S T U D Y · E L E V E N

HOW FAMILIES SPEND LEISURE TIME

Attractions visited in a six-month period

Location	Sept 86 (%)	Jan 89 (%)	Location	Sept 86 (%)	Jan 89 (%)
Shopping, garden centre	41	58	Zoo	7	15
Seaside resort	42	50	Large exhibition	7	15
Museum	14	24	Country show	8	12
Stately home, castle	14	23	Wildlife, safari park	10	11
Theme, leisure park	8	20	Art gallery	n/a	9
National park	16	20	Special interest	5	9
Sports event	17	19	Activity centre	4	7

A big tobacco company has decided to branch out into the leisure industry. It has carried out a market-research survey to find out which kinds of leisure activities are most popular.

It is also studying the results of other surveys like one carried out by the market-research firm Mintel (shown above). This was based on a sample of 884 adults who were asked about their leisure activities in the six months up to January 1989. The results were then compared with a previous survey carried out in 1986.

ACTIVITIES

Questions
1 Would it be a good idea for the tobacco company to go into the leisure industry? Explain your reasons.

2 Which activity has shown the biggest percentage rise in the period?

Report
Write a report recommending which kind, or kinds, of leisure business the company should go into, stating all your reasons.

Discussion
If you were carrying out a market-research survey into leisure activities, what essential questions would you have to ask?

Team Work
Design a market-research questionnaire which would provide information like that in the table above.

24

A Sweeter Fragrance?

Designation of Fragrances in USA

(approximate)

	% oils and essences
Perfume	20–30
Eau de parfum	10–18
Eau de Cologne	6–10
Eau de toilette	4–5

London Perfumes Ltd
Annual Sales

Name	Type	Price £	Size ml	1990	1991	1992[1]
					thousands	
Stunning	Eau de Toilette	3.99	50	90	74	63
Risky	Eau de Cologne	5.99	50	70	58	52
Allure	Eau de Parfum	14.95	30	23	28	30
Deception	Perfume	26.99	25	11	12	13

[1]Forecast sales.

The turnover of London Perfumes Ltd, which exports 25 per cent of its production to the United States, has fallen for the last two years. Forecasts for the current year show that turnover is likely to fall even further.

The main problem is that there are now so many different brands of cheap eau de toilette and eau de Cologne on the market that competition has greatly increased. As a result, the firm's market share of these types of perfume, which have the biggest volume sales, has fallen.

Steady Rise

On the other hand, sales of its more expensive eau de parfum and perfume have both shown a small, but steady rise, which is forecast to continue.

The Marketing Director has called a meeting of the Purchasing Manager, the Production Controller and the managers in her own department to discuss what actions they can take.

During their discussion, the Marketing Director has proposed that they should concentrate more on the market segment for eau de parfum, where their own brand, Allure, has shown a most encouraging increase in sales.

Purchasing Manager:	Yes, I'm all in favour of that. I tell you what we could do. At present we use 16 per cent of oils and essences in Allure. What if we reduced them to 13 or 14 per cent? That would reduce our costs.
Marketing Director:	What effect would that have on the fragrance?
Production Controller:	We could get away with 14 per cent. Most people wouldn't even notice the difference.
Export Sales Manager:	I like it! We could still officially sell Allure in the States as an eau de parfum.
Home Sales Manager:	What if we went right up market and tried to boost the sales of Deception?
Marketing Director:	No way! We're far too small to compete with the big international houses in that segment.

ACTIVITIES

Questions

1 What is meant in the case study by the following phrases:

(a) turnover

(b) market share

(c) biggest volume sales

(d) market segment

(e) up market?

2 What effect would a reduction in costs have on gross profit?

3 In your view, is the plan to concentrate more on a different market segment likely to succeed? Give your reasons.

Natasha's Plan

Natasha's Personal Expenses
Annual Estimates

	£
Clothes	350
Dry cleaning	100
Travel	200
Leisure centre	100
Evening classes	50
Holidays	450
Other expenses (eg entertainment, meals, make-up, presents, magazines)	1,000
	2,250

Natasha's Business Expenses
Annual Estimates

	£
Travel	500
Advertising	750
Telephone	150
Sunday market fees	750
Materials	1,500
Own wages	2,250
Other expenses (eg postage, stationery)	500
	6,400

Natasha had always liked making designer knitwear – partly because her mother had a shop which sold knitting wools and trimmings.

Other people had always admired the sweaters she made. They were so popular that she had already knitted sweaters for several friends in her spare time.

Worked in Bank

After she left school, Natasha worked in a bank for three years; but she never really liked it. So she decided to work for herself instead, making designer knitwear at home.

She planned to sell her knitwear through her mother's shop; by advertising in local newspapers; and at a Sunday covered market.

Her mother was very keen on the idea, and told Natasha that she need not pay her anything for living at home for the first year to see if she could make the business work.

Natasha decided to find out what prices she could charge for her knitwear. Although she had never liked working in the bank, the training she had received proved very useful in working out the figures

Personal Expenses

First of all, she wrote down her estimated personal expenses for the year to find out how much she would have to pay herself in wages. Then she wrote down what her estimated business expenses would be.

She then used a couple of formulas to work out the cost + price, based on the cost of each item plus profit.

Natasha estimated that her total sales for the first year would be 150 sweaters. She divided her total business expenses (which included her wages of £2,250) by the number of sweaters to find the cost of each sweater, ie

$$\frac{£6,400}{150} = £42.66$$

25 Per Cent Profit

Natasha decided that she wanted to make 25% profit so that she could develop the business. She used another formula to find out how much that would be for each sweater, ie

$$\frac{£42.66 \times 25}{100} = £10.66$$

By adding the two figures together, she found the total price she would have to charge for each sweater, ie

$$£42.66 + £10.66 = £53.32$$

Natasha was not too pleased with the results, as the price was too high for the market. She would have liked to have charged well under £50 so that she would have an edge on her many competitors.

She knew that if she wanted to have a lower selling price, she would have to reduce either her profit margin or her personal or business expenses.

ACTIVITIES

Questions

1 How should Natasha reduce her selling price? Explain your reasons in full, and illustrate your answer with revised accounts for personal and business expenses and pricing calculations.

2 Natasha had decided to use a penetration price to enter the market. What other kind of pricing policy could she have used? What would have been its main advantage and disadvantage?

The Best Buy?

The main hobbies of a couple, with two young children, are gardening and DIY. Six months ago, the wife was left £90,000 by her father. They have decided to give up their jobs and to live on their hobbies by buying a garden centre/DIY business.

When they have sold their house and paid off the rest of the mortgage, they will have £150,000 to invest. They do not mind where they live, or how hard they work.

They have chosen three businesses which interest them, and write off for further details. They find that the net profits of the businesses are:

Yorkshire	£16,000
West Country	£33,600
London suburb	£22,400

Only £100,000 freehold. Thriving garden centre/DIY in busy Yorkshire market town. Attractive well-fitted shop. Unopposed position. Turnover £80,000 a year. Gross profit £28,000. Excellent three-bedroom flat above premises. Scope for expansion.

Unique opportunity to purchase a substantial garden centre, plus DIY section and café in the West Country. Residential and tourist trade. Projected turnover for current year £280,000 at 30% gross profit. Large comfortable house in grounds. Freehold £300,000 (60% mortgage might be arranged).

Profitable garden centre and DIY shop in busy London suburb. Ideal for husband and wife team. Six-day trading. Present turnover £140,000. Gross profit £35,000. Spacious living accommodation above shop, comprising three bedrooms, lounge, dining room, office. £150,000 freehold.

ACTIVITIES

1 What are the gross profits of each business in figures and as a percentage?

2 What are the net profits of each business in figures and as a percentage?

3 Why does net profit give a truer picture of profitability than gross profit?

4 Which business would you advise the couple to buy? Explain your reasons in full.

Gross profit as a percentage of sales

$$\frac{\text{gross profit} \times 100}{\text{turnover}}$$

Net profit as a percentage of sales

$$\frac{\text{net profit} \times 100}{\text{turnover}}$$

Cost-Cutting Exercise

Mick Whitehill runs a small taxi firm in a country town. To save costs, he does all of the servicing and many of the smaller repairs to the three taxis himself. His profit and loss account for the previous year was as follows.

Mick Whitehill's Profit and Loss Account

	£	£
Gross profit		60,000
Less costs		
Rent	2,400	
Business rates	1,000	
Wages	21,000	
Interest on loan	2,300	
Depreciation	6,250	
Repairs	4,000	
Tax and insurance	2,100	
Hackney carriage licences	450	
Diesel fuel	7,500	
Net profit	13,000	
	60,000	60,000

ACTIVITIES

Questions

1 Which are

(a) the fixed costs

(b) the variable costs?

State the total amount of each.

2 What are the fixed costs as a percentage of the total costs?

Mick thinks that he is not making much of a net profit for all his long hours of work.

One of the problems is that the taxis are standing idle too much of the time. Furthermore, one of them has come to the end of its useful life. It is so old that it often needs expensive repairs.

He has decided that he might be better off if he got rid of the old taxi – and a driver.

If he did so, he has calculated that his gross profit would be reduced to £49,000.

On the other hand, his costs would be considerably reduced. He would save £7,000 a year on wages alone, and £2,000 on repairs.

There would also be other savings: depreciation would be reduced to £5,000; tax and insurance to £1,250; the hackney carriage licences to £300; and the fuel bill to £5,600.

ACTIVITIES

Question   Would it be sensible for Mick to get rid of a taxi and a driver? Illustrate your answer with a new profit and loss account, using Mick's estimated figures.

INFORMATION TECHNOLOGY
TRAINING CENTRE

This purpose-built centre, fully equipped with the latest IT equipment, is now offering a range of full-time courses. The classes are small, so that each student will have the maximum amount of hands-on experience under personal supervision.

The expert tutors have all had many years of practical experience in industry or commerce. Their skills will be of invaluable benefit to beginners and working people alike.

The first three courses on offer are:

Database Course   A six-day, intensive course in databases using dBASE 4. Suitable for qualified operators who have been using other software.
Price   £135

Spreadsheet Course   An introductory twelve-day course in spreadsheets, using Supercalc 5.
Price   £240

Office Skills   A ten-week (60 days) course providing a complete introduction to word processing. Choice of Word Perfect 5 or WordStar Professional 5. Suitable for beginners who want to obtain a satisfying and financially rewarding job in industry or commerce.
Price   £1,050

All prices include VAT, coursebooks and stationery

CENTRE OPENS 1 SEPTEMBER

Why not make a visit to see what we have on offer?

No appointment needed   No obligation

The Information Technology Centre will be open six days a week. The fixed costs per year are £58,400; and the variable costs per student are £12. By 31 August, the Centre had obtained the following firm bookings for its courses:

Database Course   2

Spreadsheet Course   1

Office Skills   7

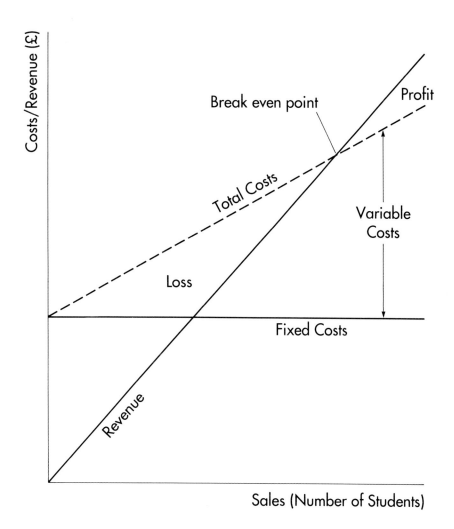

Costs/Revenue (£)

Break even point

Profit

Total Costs

Variable Costs

Loss

Fixed Costs

Revenue

Sales (Number of Students)

ACTIVITIES

Questions

1 What are the fixed costs per day?

2 What is the average sales price per student per day?

3 In your view, is the Centre likely to succeed? Illustrate your answer with a break-even chart.

Discussion What courses could the Centre have offered to other market segments which might have been more popular?

Team Work Design a new advertisement of the same size as the one above, giving details of the new courses on offer. (In your team, you will need someone to write the copy, or the words, in the advertisement; someone to plan the layout and design; someone to draw illustrations; and a team leader.)

Gerry Patten's Cash-Flow Forecast

	March		April		May		June	
	Projected £	Actual £	Projected £	Actual £	Projected £	Actual £	Projected £	Actual £
Receipts								
Sales–cash	800	900	900	1,000	850	760	950	
Sales–debtors	1,250	800	1,000	850	1,400	640	1,150	
Total receipts	2,050	1,700	1,900	1,850	2,250	1,400	2,100	
Payments								
Cash purchases	1,200	1,200	1,250	1,300	1,300	1,400	1,200	
Creditors	100	200	200	150	100	300	200	
Others	550	500	550	560	550	600	500	
Total payments	1,850	1,900	2,000	2,010	1,950	2,300	1,900	
Receipts ± payments	200	(200)	(100)	(160)	300	(900)	200	
Opening bank balance	(1,000)	(1,000)	(800)	(1,200)	(900)	(1,360)	(600)	
Closing bank balance	(800)	(1,200)	(900)	(1,360)	(600)	(2,260)	(400)	

Gerry Patten is a self-employed decorator and builder who employs casual workers if he has a job to do which he cannot handle by himself. His wife, Dawn, who was trained as a bookkeeper, handles the financial side of the business.

Gerry buys practically all of his materials for cash at a local builder's yard, where he receives a small trade discount.

Appeals for Payment

Some of his customers pay in cash. Dawn sends out monthly bills to the other customers. A few of them pay promptly, but she often has to wait for months to receive a cheque, in spite of repeated appeals for payment.

Gerry relies on a small bank overdraft to provide his working capital. His overdraft usually increases in the winter when bad weather often stops him from doing much outside work. However, his overdraft has increased greatly this spring when it was forecast to fall.

The bank manager has asked Gerry and Dawn to make an appointment to see him.

National Westminster Bank PLC   Cashflow Forecast For   For the period

| Branch | | name of company, firm etc | | | | | | | | | | From | To | | |

Enter month

	Projected	Actual	Projected	Actual	Projected	Actual	Projected	Actual	Projected	Actual	Projected	Actual	Total Projected	Total Actual
Receipts														
Sales – Cash														
Sales – Debtors														
Loans														
Other receipts														
A Total receipts														
Payments														
Cash purchases														
To creditors														
Wages and salaries (net)														
PAYE/NIC														
Capital items														
Rent/rates														
Services														
HP/leasing repayments														
Bank/finance charges														
Loan repayments														
VAT (net)														
Corporation tax, etc														
Dividend														
B Total payments														
Opening bank balance														
Add to B if overdrawn Subtract from B if credit														
C Total														
D Closing bank balance (Difference between A&C)														

ACTIVITIES

Questions

1 What is the meaning in the case study of

   (a) overdraft

   (b) working capital?

2 How does Gerry pay for most of his materials?

3 What are the total actual cash and actual credit sales for the period from March to May?

4 What, on average, are actual credit sales as a percentage of total actual sales during the three-month period?

5 What is the greatest error in the cash-flow forecast for May? Why, in your view, did this occur?

6 If you were the bank manager, what advice would you give Gerry and Dawn?

7 Use this advice to draw up a new cash-flow forecast for June and July, showing the projected figures, but leaving the actual figures blank.

A Helpful Bank Manager

Short-Term Loan at 12%

Monthly Repayments

Repayment period	Amount of loan		
	£ 1,000	£ 2,000	£ 3,000
One year	88.69	173.38	266.07
Two years	46.92	93.84	140.76
Three years	33.07	66.14	99.21

Karen had decided to give up her job as a teacher of business studies and set up her own secretarial agency instead. She intended to work from home at first, and then rent an office when she could afford it.

A friend of hers had done the same thing, and two years later she was earning much more than she had ever earned in teaching.

£2,000 loan

Karen and her husband John, who was a personnel officer in a large firm, had used the same bank for a number of years. They knew the bank manager quite well as he had helped them to arrange a mortgage to buy their home.

She made an appointment with the bank manager to see if she could obtain a £2,000 loan to buy a computer, software and a printer.

The bank manager was very helpful. He told her that she could borrow £2,000, or £3,000 if she wanted to buy other equipment, for a period of one to two years. He did not even ask for any security on the loan; but then he knew that John had a good job, and that they were both careful with their money.

Business Plan

Before Karen left, he advised her to draw up a business plan, as it would help to get her business off to a flying start. He told her that the main features of a business plan were:

▶ aims and objectives
▶ markets and selling plans
▶ financial analysis and prospects
▶ administration.

ACTIVITIES

Questions

1 Would you advise Karen to take out a bigger loan for £3,000? Explain your reasons.

2 Work out the total repayments for a period of one year and two years for *either* a £2,000 loan *or* a £3,000 loan if you have chosen that amount. What is the difference in the total repayments over one year and two years?

3 State which period you would advise Karen to choose, explaining your reasons.

Team Work

Draw up a business plan for a person who is starting a local secretarial agency, using the headings listed in the case study.

Lease or Hire?

A firm of paint manufacturers has decided to sell its ageing fleet of company cars and replace them with a new fleet of 30 hired or leased Sapphire 1.6Ls. It has received the following quotation of the monthly payments for each car over a three-year period (36 payments):

Contract Hire		Lease
With maintenance	Without maintenance	
£200	£180	£190

Contract hire with maintenance includes the road-fund licence, all servicing, mechanical repairs and RAC subscription.

Contract hire without maintenance provides only the road-fund licence. The firm would be responsible for all servicing and repairs.

Leasing provides none of these benefits; but at the end of the three-year period the firm receives 40 per cent of the residual value of the cars, or the price for which they are sold.

ACTIVITIES

Questions

1 What would be the main advantage for the firm in hiring or leasing the fleet instead of buying the cars itself?

2 What would be the total cost over the three-year period of:

   (a) hiring the cars with maintenance

   (b) hiring them without maintenance

   (c) leasing them?

3 Which method would you recommend the firm to choose? State your reasons in full.

Balance Sheet at 31 December – current year

	£m	£m	£m
Fixed assets			
Land and buildings		10	
Plant and equipment		8	
			18
Current assets			
Stock	32		
Debtors	26		
Cash in hand and at bank	1		
		59	
Current liabilities			
Creditors	40		
Overdraft and loans	9		
Taxes	1		
		50	
			9
			27
Net assets			
Represented by:			
Ordinary shares		23	
Reserves		4	
			27

Balance Sheet at 31 December – previous year

	£m	£m	£m
Fixed assets			
Land and buildings		9	
Plant and equipment		7	
			16
Current assets			
Stock	20		
Debtors	30		
Cash in hand and at bank	6		
		56	
Current liabilities			
Creditors	30		
Overdraft and loans	4		
Taxes	1		
		35	
			21
			37
Net assets			
Represented by:			
Ordinary shares		20	
Reserves		17	
			37

A firm of builders' merchants has had big problems during the last financial year. The fall in house building has greatly reduced sales. At the same time, the firm has had to face much fiercer competition from bigger British and other European Community companies in the run-up to 1992.

As a result, its net profits have fallen from £4m in the previous year to £500,000 in the current year.

The firm's balance sheets for the two years shows that it has serious financial problems.

ACTIVITIES

Questions

1 By how much has stock increased during the year?

2 If all the creditors wanted the firm to pay off its debts, would the firm be able to do so? Illustrate your answer with a ratio.

3 State whether the firm has been efficient in managing its business. Illustrate your answer with a ratio for the current and the previous year.

Report

Use the information in the balance sheets to write a report explaining in full how the firm has tried to cope with its fall in revenue. Suggest what actions it might have taken instead.

Current ratio

$$\frac{\text{current assets}}{\text{current liabilities}}$$

Acid test

$$\frac{\text{current assets} - \text{stock}}{\text{current liabilities}}$$

Net return on capital employed

$$\frac{\text{net profit}}{\text{total capital employed}} \times 100$$

Orchard Cottage
Newball
Southshire
SY2 AE,

The Advertising Standards
    Authority L.T.D.
Torrington Place
London
WC1E 7HN

Dear Sirs,
            I wish to protest in the strongest possible terms about the enclosed advertisement which I consider to be totally misleading, as the quoted prices do not include V.A.T.
    Although this fact is mentioned, it is tucked away at the bottom of the advertisement in very small type so that some readers may not notice it. In contrast, 'free delivery' is displayed very prominently.
    The advertisement asks readers to 'compare our prices,' but this would be difficult for people who do not know the present rate of V.A.T.
    It would also be difficult to work out 15% of £28.50 if you do not have a calculator handy!
    I consider that this advertisement is a deliberate attempt to deceive. I would be grateful if you would give the matter your urgent attention.
                            Yours faithfully,
                            John Smith

MISLEADING ADVERTISEMENTS: NEW REGULATIONS

New regulations aimed at protecting the interests of consumers, traders and the general public from the effects of misleading advertisements came into force in 1988. The Director General's role under the regulations is to support and reinforce existing advertising controls, not to replace them. The regulations give him the power to step in if the public interest requires that advertisements complained of should be stopped by means of a court injunction.

Although the Director General may have power to intervene, the bulk of complaints will continue to be handled through existing channels – called established means *in the regulations. The main ones are:*

TRADING STANDARDS (OR CONSUMER PROTECTION) DEPARTMENTS
which enforce the Trade Descriptions Act and other consumer laws. The departments are to be found in London boroughs, metropolitan boroughs, in county councils and Scottish regional and island councils. In Northern Ireland the Trading Standards Branch is part of the Department of Economic Development. See area phone books for addresses.

ACTIVITIES

Questions
1 Name two bodies which deal with complaints about misleading advertisements. State briefly what powers they have.

2 Do you consider that John Smith's complaint about the advertisement is justified? Explain your reasons in full.

3 If you think the advertisement should be altered, state what changes should be made.

Discussion
Are the controls over illegal, misleading or offensive advertisements strict enough?

Advertising Campaign

C A S E · S T U D Y · T W E N T Y · T W O

An airline is starting a new service of business flights from Heathrow Airport to other European Community countries.

The advertising agency which handles the airline's account has been given a budget of £400,000 for the advertising campaign. It will be targeted on business people in the London area.

Siobhan, who is in charge of the campaign, has already decided how she will spend most of the budget. She has decided to buy:

▶ Six full-page advertisements in the *Financial Times* in a special position on the first right-hand page at £23,700 each   £142,200

▶ five 30-second spots in the breaks in *News at Ten* on Thames Television at £43,000 each   £215,000

That leaves her with £42,800 to spend. She had decided to spend the whole amount on 60-second spot advertisements on Capital Radio during one week. She is studying Capital Radio's rate card, and some graphs showing the most popular listening times for the ABC1 adults that she wants to reach.

ACTIVITIES

Questions

1 Why in your view did Siobhan choose to advertise in the *Financial Times* and in the breaks in *News at Ten*?

2 What percentage of the total budget is being spent on advertising in newspapers, on television, and on radio?

3 Do you think the proportions spent in each of the three media is right or wrong? Explain your reasons in full.

4 Look at Capital Radio's Standard Rates and Rate Card Segments tables. Which are the most expensive and the cheapest time segments? Why do you think there is such a big difference in the rates?

Standard Rates

Spots will be divided between the days covered and will be rotated within the appropriate time segment of each day.

Subject to availability, Advertisers' day and time preferences can be fixed upon payment of a fixing charge.

Prices for longer time lengths are discounted as the ratio below shows. Spots of longer duration than 60 seconds are charged pro-rata to the 60 second rate.

TIME SEGMENT (RATIO)	60″ (180)	50″ (165)	40″ (130)	30″ (100)	20″ (80)	10″ (50)
P1	£2700	£2480	£1950	£1500	£1200	£ 750
P2	£1350	£1240	£ 980	£ 750	£ 600	£ 380
A	£ 720	£ 660	£ 520	£ 400	£ 320	£ 200
B	£ 360	£ 330	£ 260	£ 200	£ 160	£ 100
C	£ 90	£ 85	£ 65	£ 50	£ 40	£ 25

Rate Card Segments

TIME SEGMENT	MONDAY-FRIDAY	SATURDAY	SUNDAY
P1	0700–1100	0700–1200	1000–1300
P2	0600–0700 1100–1700	1200–1700 –	0700–1000 –
A	1700–2000	–	1300–1900
B	2000–2400	0600–0700 1700–2400	1900–2400 –
C	0000–0600 (M-F AM)	0000–0600 (AM)	0000–0700 (AM)

5 At which times on an average weekday do most ABC1 adults listen to Capital Radio? What in your view is the reason?

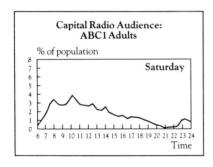
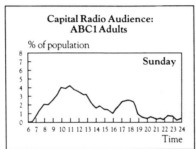
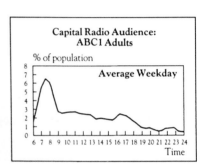

Source: Capital Radio 1988

6 Make out a table showing how Siobhan should spend the £42,800 on 60-second spots during the week. (Ignore VAT in your calculations.) Explain why you have chosen to spend the money in that way.

Changing the Image

THE COMPARATIVE IMAGE OF THE POTATO

The image of the potato as compared with other food was examined.

The potato is seen to be reliable, dependable, and part of the British way of life.

However, the potato is seen to be a necessity rather than something that is exciting or particularly modern. In addition, despite its healthy image, it is also seen as somewhat fattening.

The jacket potato, however, is nearer to the image of rice and pasta. It is seen as young, healthy, fun and even exciting.

People were asked about different types of food which are high in carbohydrate.

Potatoes were considered to be natural (91 per cent) and traditional (91 per cent). They were also seen to be nutritious (81 per cent) and versatile, or capable of being used in different ways (81 per cent).

They were seen to be less fattening than pasta or bread, but not less fattening than rice.

There were some differences in the image of potatoes amongst different class groups. In particular ABC1s were significantly more likely that C2DEs to say that potatoes 'are particularly high in fibre', have 'a good balance of vitamins', and that they 'are not particularly fattening'.

Source: Potato Marketing Board, Potatoes (adapted)

ASSOCIATED ADVERTISING PLC MEMORANDUM	
To: Daniel Downton	Date: 2 August
From: Beth Mills	Reference: bm/ka
Subject: Potato Image	
Please let me have a report on how we can create a better image for potatoes, particularly among young people.	

ACTIVITIES

Questions

1 What are the main rival foods to potatoes?

2 What are the main differences in attitudes to potatoes between different class groups?

3 Which way of serving potatoes has the most modern image? In your view, what are the main reasons?

Report Write a report explaining how you would improve the image of potatoes among young people.

Discussion If you were in charge of a £1 million advertising budget for potatoes, how much, if any, would you spend on advertising in the following media:

Television

Radio

Sunday newspapers

Daily newspapers

Magazines

Cinema screens

Street posters

Team Work Design an advertisement for a tabloid newspaper, such as the *Sun*, to improve the image of potatoes. (In your team, you will need someone to write the copy, or the words, for the advertisement; someone to plan the layout and design; someone to draw the illustrations; and a team leader.)

A Grand Opening

Mohammed Siddiqui is opening a sports shop and wants to get his business off to a good start. In his business plan, he has budgeted £1,000 for a grand opening. He has jotted down some ideas about publicity for the launch of his business – and their costs.

	Cost
A Opening sales offer with 10 per cent off all prices. Estimated sales £4,000.	£400
B Thirty-second spots in off-peak time on local radio. Each spot:	£100
C Opening ceremony by local mayor, who is also chairman of the local cricket team.	Free
D Display advertisements in local newspaper. Each advertisement:	£200
E Karate demonstration by a local man, who has represented England, and his students.	£100
F Opening of the shop by a famous footballer.	£1,000

G Door-to-door leaflet drop at £35 per thousand, plus A5 colour leaflets at:
£130 per 1,000
£140 per 2,000
£165 per 5,000
£250 per 10,000

Cost according to quantity

Mohammed has decided that if he uses a door-to-door drop of leaflets, he wants blanket coverage of the area, so he will have 10,000 leaflets delivered.

ACTIVITIES

Questions

1 What would be the total cost of printing and delivering 10,000 leaflets?

2 Draw up a publicity budget showing how you think Mohammed should spend his £1,000. (You can include any number of radio spots or display advertisements, so long as the total budget does not exceed £1,000.)

3 Explain in full why you have chosen to spend the money in that way, and why you did not choose the other methods.

4 What other kinds of publicity might Mohammed have used for the launch of his shop? What would have been their main advantages?

Job Vacancy

An expanding firm of insurance brokers wants to recruit a customer services assistant for its front counter. It has put the following display advertisement in a newspaper.

CUSTOMER SERVICES ASSISTANT

Young customer services assistant needed for front counter in friendly insurance broker's office.

You will be the sort of person who likes a varied and busy day. You will find yourself handling telephone and personal enquiries and our electronic terminals; advising customers on the range of services we offer; and handling cash and cheques. In addition, you will carry out routine office and general word processing duties.

We are looking for someone who is 18+, with a good educational background in English and mathematics, and accurate keyboarding. Full training will be given in our word processing and database systems – WordStar 4 and dBase 4. You will need to have a pleasant, outgoing personality and be capable of working as a member of a team whose work load can be quite hectic at times.

In return, we provide an attractive salary, a yearly bonus, free life insurance, profit-sharing pension scheme, and 20 days annual holiday.

We are an equal opportunities employer.

The firm received three replies.
The main details of each applicant were:

Amanda Johnson
Age: 18

Education:
Comprehensive school

Qualifications:
GCSE English B
GCSE Maths C

Keyboarding speeds:
30 wpm

Hobbies:
Swimming
Carpentry

Singh Anand
Age: 20

Education:
College of technology

Qualifications:
A level English
BTEC Diploma in Business and Finance

Keyboarding speeds:
60 wpm

Hobbies:
Computers
Volleyball

Natalie White
Age: 19

Education:
Private schools

Qualifications:
GCSE English C
GCSE Maths F

Keyboarding speeds:
40 wpm

Hobbies:
Horseriding
Scuba diving

All three applicants were called in for an interview. During the interviews, the owner of the firm made the following notes:

Amanda Johnson:—

Very hesitant
Never looks you straight in the eye
Dirty fingernails

Singh Anand :—

Quiet, but confident
Rather serious

Natalie White :-

Very pleasant manner
Smiles a lot
Expensive clothes

ACTIVITIES

Questions

1 What is meant by the phrase 'an equal opportunities employer' in the advertisement?

2 Use the information in the advertisement to write a job description for the post of customer services assistant.

3 In your view, which applicant should be given the job, or should the post be re-advertised? Explain your reasons in full.

Business Growth Training

C A S E · S T U D Y · T W E N T Y · S I X

An expanding chain of cafés in the Midlands, which employs 900 people in all, has decided to set up its own training scheme for its 650 waiters and waitresses and kitchen staff. The main purpose is to improve standards of hygiene and customer care.

The Personnel Department has decided to use a small learning pack of case studies which will be produced by the department itself. These will be distributed free to each of the 650 employees.

This will be supported by a video made by a specialist training firm. The video will be used at the central training centre on courses for managers and on induction courses for new employees.

The firm has applied to the Training Agency for help under Option 5 of its Business Growth Training programme.

How to implement your own innovative training solution

Option 5 aims to encourage the development of innovative training – to help your company tackle the new challenges of the 1990's with new training approaches. Also central to Option 5 is your involvement in spreading the benefits of new approaches to other businesses.

How does Option 5 work?

Chances are, if you've given any thought to your company's training needs, you'll have come up with a few ideas of your own – some of which may be quite radical.

If you have any original training ideas in mind, or if you feel a different approach to your training would be of more benefit to your business, then the Training Agency can help you turn it into a reality.

How the Training Agency can help

Setting up an entirely new programme isn't easy – especially when you're attempting something that hasn't been done before. That's why the Training Agency is prepared to provide your business with help in a variety of ways.

They'll provide you with training specialists to advise you at no charge on your particular scheme. And, as with some of the other training options in this brochure, the Training Agency is prepared to offer financial help if the design of your particular training approach qualifies. They'll also pay you to tell other businesses about the benefits of your new approach.

During your project, the Training Agency will help you measure your progress and pay-back. So, not only can you measure the results, you can also justify your own investment.

"We developed low cost open learning packs to achieve better customer care standards"

Which companies benefit?

If your company employs under 1,000 staff and you would be unable to go ahead with your new training approach without help from the Training Agency, Option 5 is ideal for you. (Companies with over 1,000 employees can also receive help under certain circumstances.)

So if you'd like to take a fresh look at training, simply complete and return the enclosed reply-card.

bgt

BUSINESS GROWTH TRAINING

ACTIVITIES

Questions

1 What benefits could the firm receive from the Training Agency?

2 Do you think the Personnel Department has chosen the most suitable training methods? Explain your reasons.

3 Would you advise the firm to tell other companies about its new training scheme? What would be the main advantages and disadvantages?

Team Work   Write a case study for the learning pack which would improve the ways in which waiters and waitresses deal with customers. (In your team, you will need someone to write the words; someone to plan the layout and design; someone to draw the illustrations; and a team leader.)

49

Headhunters

Sarah Browne works for a firm of headhunters which recruits very senior managers for client firms. Her current target is a 40-year-old marketing manager in a northern brewery.

A London firm which makes a well-known brand of soft drink has asked Sarah to try to recruit him as their marketing manager to help fight off the competition from other European Community firms that 1992 is expected to bring.

Sarah has spent the last month investigating her target. She has found out how much he earns and the fringe benefits he receives – an annual 10% bonus; a company car; a non-contributory pension scheme; medical and life assurance cover; and a mortgage subsidy.

The soft drinks firm has agreed to increase his salary by 20 per cent, and to provide a generous relocation package and all the fringe benefits that he already receives. It is also willing to provide other fringe benefits if they will persuade him to take the job.

Future Fears

During her detailed investigations, Sarah has discovered what her target likes and fears the most.

Although he has very little time for relaxation, he loves going to the opera and sailing. Despite his high salary, he has a great fear that when he does retire his pension will not be high enough to cover inflation, and that he will not be able to afford to keep up full medical insurance.

ACTIVITIES

Questions

1 What is meant by the following words and phrases in the case study:

(a) headhunters

(b) marketing manager

(c) 1992

(d) fringe benefits

(e) company car

(f) non-contributory pension scheme

(g) life assurance

(h) relocation package?

2 What specific fringe benefits could be provided to persuade the marketing manager to change his job?

Report

Write a report that Sarah might send to the client firm, describing the total package of fringe benefits and the advantages of each.

Discussion

Which would you prefer — higher pay or more fringe benefits?

Management Buy-out

Dunsford District Council has just decided to sell off its nursery, which supplies plants and shrubs to all the council's parks and open spaces.

When the council employees heard the news, they were angry and confused at first; but then the senior officials in the nursery decided to put in a bid so that they could run the nursery as a private company themselves.

They planned to expand the business if their bid was successful. They would go on supplying Dunsford Council with plants and shrubs, but try to sell their products to other councils as well. A garden centre would be added to the nursery; and they would also start a garden design and consultancy service. The management buy-out succeeded.

Suitable Name

Before the company could be set up, a suitable name had to be chosen. This was an important matter, as the name was the basic means of creating a good image in the outside world.

The three people who would be the directors of the new company were meeting to discuss the question.

Adrian: We can't use 'Dunsford Council' any more, but I think we ought to keep 'Dunsford' in the name. We've won a lot of prizes in horticultural shows all over the country, so we're quite well known. We should try to build on that. I suggest we call the company 'Dunsford Nursery Supplies Ltd'.

Sally: That's a bit narrow, Adrian. After all, we're going to provide much more than plants and shrubs now. I think we ought to call the company something like 'Dunsford Park and Garden Services'.

Murtala: I don't agree. Those names are far too dull. The whole gardening scene has changed in the last few years. We want a name which is more modern and appealing – something which will give a fun image. What about 'Blooming Good!' or 'Growth Unlimited'? Just think of the logo you could make out of those!

ACTIVITIES

Questions

1 What is the meaning of 'management buy-out' in the case study?

2 In your view, which of the names suggested in the case study is most suitable? Explain your reasons in full.

3 Design a suitable logo to go with the name you have chosen.

Micro Merge

In a secret deal, Turnkey, a major firm of computer system designers, has just bought a small software house which employs 24 people. Turnkey's main purpose is to obtain access to the skills of the brilliant team of software programmers in the smaller firm, in particular those of two young women. It would like to transfer them to its own company.

Apart from that, Turnkey has no intention of altering the way in which the software house is run, or of dismissing any employees.

However, it knows that any takeover can cause anxiety, and often resentment. It hopes to avoid that by providing all employees with a new company bonus scheme, based on annual results, which could add from 5 per cent to 9 per cent to their salaries.

Turnkey's management has had long discussions about the ways in which the news of the takeover should be communicated to the employees of the software house. It is still considering a number of options. They are:

▶ to let the Managing Director of the software house communicate the news to the staff in his own way

▶ to send each employee a personal letter giving the news

▶ to flash up an announcement on the computer screens of all employees announcing the takeover, and asking them to access a file entitled 'Read Me' for further details

▶ to put up printed posters announcing the takeover

▶ to hold a meeting of the whole staff which would be addressed by Turnkey's Managing Director

▶ to approach the two young women first – in secret

ACTIVITIES

Questions

1 Which method of communication would you advise Turnkey to use? Explain your reasons.

2 Write an announcement of the takeover which could be flashed up on the computer screens.

Change of Ownership

Matthew worked as a fork-lift-truck driver in a small distribution firm. His basic wage for a 40-hour week was £4 an hour. Except when he was on his annual three-week holiday, he also worked an average of three hours overtime a week. The rate for overtime was time and a half.

When a much bigger company took over the firm, the workers feared that some of them would lose their jobs and be made redundant. Rumours swept through the firm that wages were going to be cut.

Management Proposals

Nothing happened for a while, but then the new management called a meeting with the shop stewards and convenors. Management explained their proposals for a new wages structure.

Shortly after that, all workers received a letter describing the new scheme. Further details were given in the works newsletter that had just been started.

Matthew found that he would now be paid an annual salary of £8,300 a year for a 40-hour week. No overtime would be worked.

In addition, he would receive a guaranteed bonus of 10 per cent, and even more if he exceeded his productivity target.

There would also be a company-wide productivity bonus, linked to the company's total performance. This bonus ranged from £50 to £250 a year in the new owner's other branches.

All the workers had been asked to vote on the new proposals. Matthew didn't want to vote just as his union told him, so he decided to work out for himself how the wages offer would affect him.

ACTIVITIES

Questions

1 Under the old system, what were Matthew's basic wages a year?

2 What were his total wages for a year including payments for overtime?

3 Under the new system, what would be the minimum amount he would receive in a year?

4 Would you advise Matthew to vote for the new system? Explain your reasons in full.

All Out!

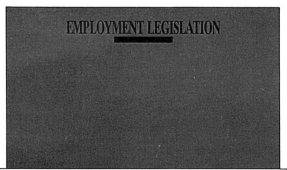

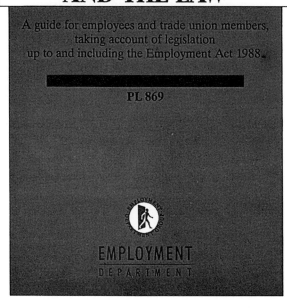

EMPLOYMENT LEGISLATION

INDUSTRIAL ACTION
AND THE LAW

A guide for employees and trade union members,
taking account of legislation
up to and including the Employment Act 1988.

PL 869

EMPLOYMENT
D E P A R T M E N T

Employees who take industrial action will know that there may be damaging financial consequences for them, since they are unlikely to receive any pay if they withdraw their labour. They should also be aware that they may be putting their jobs at risk . . .

A union must not organise or induce industrial action unless it has held a ballot . . .

The date of the ballot may not be more than four weeks before the start of the industrial action . . .

In the past union members have been disciplined by their unions for working during a strike or other industrial action, but union members should be allowed to make up their own minds whether or not to take (or continue) industrial action . . .

Section 3 of the 1988 Act makes union discipline unjustifiable in such circumstances . . .

An individual has been disciplined by a union where one or more of the following penalties has been imposed:

- expulsion from the union or from any branch or section of it

- payment of a sum of money (for example, as a fine) to the union.

Common examples of conduct for which individuals are protected against unjustifiable discipline are:

- going to work despite a call to take strike or any other industrial action (the individual is protected whether or not there has been any kind of ballot and whatever its outcome)

- crossing any picket line (including one mounted by the individual's own union at his own place of work)

- speaking out against a call to take any strike or other industrial action.

Source: Department of Employment, Industrial Action and the Law (extracts)

A union representing hospital porters and cleaners and similar workers, had called a national strike in support of its 12 per cent pay claim. In a secret ballot three weeks before, 93 per cent of the members had voted in favour.

Sarah Cookson was one of the small minority who had voted against. She was a 41-year-old widow, with two teenage daughters to support, and worked as a cleaner in a big hospital.

She relied on her weekly wages to supplement her small widow's pension, which wasn't nearly big enough to live on. Sarah feared that if the strike went on for a long time, she would fall hopelessly into debt.

That was one of the reasons she had decided to go on working during the strike. Sarah had never been afraid of speaking her mind, and all the other cleaners knew what she intended to do.

Shop Steward's Visit

The day before the strike was due to start, she had a visit from a shop steward.

'What's all this I hear about you being a scab, Sarah?' he asked.

'I voted against the strike, and I'm not joining it. I can't afford to for a start . . .'

'We're all in the same boat. We've got to stick together if we want better wages.'

'I don't believe in strikes. I never have.'

'But you won't mind taking the 12 per cent when we get it, will you ? I've got no time for your sort in our branch. You'd better do a bit of quick thinking, or you'll find yourself without a union card.'

ACTIVITIES

Questions

1 Which Act made it lawful for Sarah not to join the strike? What other rights did the Act give her?

2 Was it lawful for the shop steward to act as he did?

3 Do you think Sarah was right to go on working? Explain your reasons in full.

Discussion

Have recent trade union laws taken away too many rights from workers?

Enterprise Centre

C A S E · S T U D Y · T H I R T Y · T W O

Tom Slater was a retired businessman who lived in a big house in a quiet country lane near the market town of Shire. He had no neighbours for a quarter-of-a-mile, apart from John King, who lived at Bridge Farm next door.

One evening, as he was glancing through the local paper, his eye was caught by an announcement. As he read it, he jerked upright in his chair.

SHIRE DISTRICT COUNCIL
TOWN AND COUNTRY
PLANNING ACT 1971

NOTICE is hereby given that the following application has been made to Shire District Council:

3/346/12 – For planning permission to demolish redundant farm buildings at Bridge Farm and for redevelopment of farmyard to provide an Enterprise Centre containing twenty workshops for small businesses.

A copy of the application and of the plans and other documents submitted with it may be inspected during normal office hours at the Planning Office, Shire District Council, High Road, Shire.

Any person who wishes to make representations about the application should do so by writing to me within 21 days of the date of this notice, quoting the above reference number.

J A F HUTTON
Chief Executive Officer
Shire District Council
·18 High Road
Shire TN6 1YT

'Just look at this!' Tom called to his wife Emily, handing her the newspaper. 'That John King never even had the decency to tell us what he was thinking of doing.'

'Perhaps he won't get planning permission, dear.'

'I'll see that he doesn't,' said Tom aggressively. 'If he does, we can say goodbye to our quiet life here.'

Huge Sign

At ten o'clock next morning, Tom strode into the Council Planning Office. The development was even worse than he expected. There would be a huge sign, labelled ENTERPRISE CENTRE, at the entrance, and a car park near the boundary of Tom's garden.

In support of his application, John King claimed that it would:

- provide local employment in constructing the buildings

- give local young people and the unemployed a chance to set up their own businesses

- provide useful commercial services for local residents

- encourage tourism, as some of the workshops would be used for crafts, such as hand-made toys and stained-glass windows.

Tom's Protest

When Tom returned home, he immediately sat down and wrote a letter of protest.

> Bridgefoot House,
> Bridge Lane,
> Shire
>
> Ref No. 3/346/12
> Mr J. A. F. Hutton
> Chief Executive
> Shire District Council
>
> Dear Sir,
>   I wish to protest in the strongest possible terms against the proposed development of an enterprise centre at Bridge Farm.
>   This development would completely destroy one of the most important areas of natural beauty and wildlife in the area.
>   As you know, Bridge Lane is very narrow and winding. There is little traffic at present, but the proposed development would almost certainly lead to a great increase, with risks of serious road accidents.
>   Although the Centre might help to encourage tourism, there are many wasteland sights in Shire itself which would be far more suitable and convenient for day trippers who have come by coach or train.
>   Many older residents of Shire do not own cars. They, too, would benefit far more from the commercial services, if they were provided in the town, on their own doorsteps.
>   Yours faithfully,
>
>   Tom Slater

There were no other objections to the proposed development.

ACTIVITIES

Questions

1 State two other situations in which businesses would have to apply for planning permission.

2 If you were a member of the Shire Council Planning Committee, would you support Tom's objection or not? Give your reasons.

European Loan

An expanding firm which makes plastic mouldings is setting up a new factory. The total cost of the plant and machinery will be £368,000. It is providing half of the money out of its own reserves, and is going to borrow the other half – £184,000.

The interest rate for a bank loan would be 15 per cent. The firm has written to the Welsh Development Agency (WDA) to find out whether it could get a European Coal and Steel Community (ECSC) loan if it set up the new factory in Wales. These low-cost loans are given to businesses in areas where the closing of coal mines and steel plants has created unemployment.

From the information about the loans, it seems that the firm might be able to obtain a loan of £184,000 as the factory will create 25 new jobs. However, there are many other factors which have to be taken into account before it decides whether to apply for a loan or not.

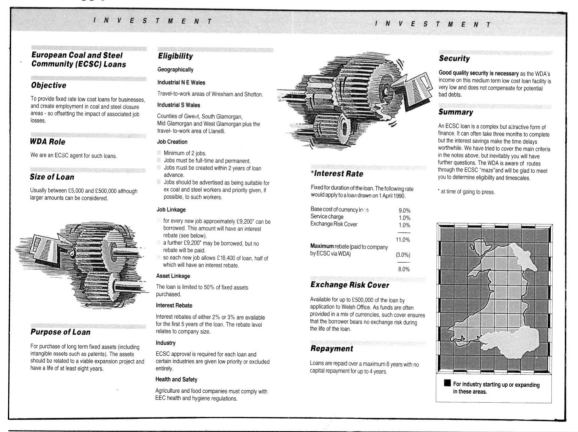

INVESTMENT   INVESTMENT

European Coal and Steel Community (ECSC) Loans

Objective

To provide fixed rate low cost loans for businesses, and create employment in coal and steel closure areas - so offsetting the impact of associated job losses.

WDA Role

We are an ECSC agent for such loans.

Size of Loan

Usually between £5,000 and £500,000 although larger amounts can be considered.

Purpose of Loan

For purchase of long term fixed assets (including intangible assets such as patents). The assets should be related to a viable expansion project and have a life of at least eight years.

Eligibility

Geographically

Industrial N E Wales

Travel-to-work areas of Wrexham and Shotton.

Industrial S Wales

Counties of Gwent, South Glamorgan, Mid Glamorgan and West Glamorgan plus the travel- to-work area of Llanelli.

Job Creation

- Minimum of 2 jobs.
- Jobs must be full-time and permanent.
- Jobs must be created within 2 years of loan advance.
- Jobs should be advertised as being suitable for ex coal and steel workers and priority given, if possible, to such workers.

Job Linkage

- for every new job approximately £9,200* can be borrowed. This amount will have an interest rebate (see below).
- a further £9,200* may be borrowed, but no rebate will be paid.
- so each new job allows £18,400 of loan, half of which will have an interest rebate.

Asset Linkage

The loan is limited to 50% of fixed assets purchased.

Interest Rebate

Interest rebates of either 2% or 3% are available for the first 5 years of the loan. The rebate level relates to company size.

Industry

ECSC approval is required for each loan and certain industries are given low priority or excluded entirely.

Health and Safety

Agriculture and food companies must comply with EEC health and hygiene regulations.

*Interest Rate

Fixed for duration of the loan. The following rate would apply to a loan drawn on 1 April 1990.

Base cost of currency loan	9.0%
Service charge	1.0%
Exchange Risk Cover	1.0%
	11.0%
Maximum rebate (paid to company by ECSC via WDA)	(3.0%)
	8.0%

Exchange Risk Cover

Available for up to £500,000 of the loan by application to Welsh Office. As funds are often provided in a mix of currencies, such cover ensures that the borrower bears no exchange risk during the life of the loan.

Repayment

Loans are repaid over a maximum 8 years with no capital repayment for up to 4 years.

Security

Good quality security is necessary as the WDA's income on this medium term low cost loan facility is very low and does not compensate for potential bad debts.

Summary

An ECSC loan is a complex but attractive form of finance. It can often take three months to complete but the interest savings make the time delays worthwhile. We have tried to cover the main criteria in the notes above, but inevitably you will have further questions. The WDA is aware of routes through the ECSC "maze" and will be glad to meet you to determine eligibility and timescales.

* at time of going to press.

■ For industry starting up or expanding in these areas.

ACTIVITIES

Questions   1   In which areas of Wales would the factory have to be sited?

2   What would be the minimum number of new jobs which would have to be created to obtain an ECSC loan for £184,000?

3   If the firm obtained an ECSC loan for £184,000, what would be the annual interest charge on the part of the loan for which it gets no rebate?

4   What would the annual interest charge be on the other half of the ECSC loan, assuming that the firm gets the maximum rebate of 3 per cent?

5   What would be the total annual interest charges for an ECSC loan?

6   What would be the annual interest charge for a bank loan of £184,000?

7   Taking all the other factors about location of business into consideration, would you advise the firm to apply for an ECSC loan or not? Explain your reasons.

Trade Deficit

'We'll have to make 10 per cent of our workforce redundant.'

Northern furniture manufacturer

BANK RATE RISES TO 15 PER CENT
£2.2 billion trade deficit in May

Daily Bugle

'The rise isn't big enough to convince foreigners. The £ is still falling.'

Bank official

'We'd better cut our orders straight away. We're already overstocked.'

A big importer

'That will be a real help to us!'

Chain of estate agents

ACTIVITIES

Questions

1 Explain in your own words:

(a) Why the furniture manufacturer had to make workers redundant

(b) Why the importer was going to reduce orders

(c) what the estate agent meant by saying that the rise in interest rates would be 'a real help to us'

(d) why the £ was still falling.

Letter

Write a letter to a newspaper explaining all the effects that a rise in interest rates would have on business. Outline other financial measures that the government might have taken instead.

61

Animal Rights

Suzanne had always believed in animal rights, though she had never been a member of any animal-rights organisation.

As she was walking along the high street one day, she saw a poster announcing that a circus which used performing animals was coming to town. She felt upset at first, and then angry.

As the days passed, her anger grew. She decided to do something about it. That evening, she wrote a short letter to the local paper criticising the use of performing animals in circuses.

When her letter was published, she was astonished by the response. Her telephone never seemed to stop ringing. Apart from one person, all her callers were against the circus visit.

She also received a number of letters of support, including one from the secretary of an animal-rights organisation in London, inviting her to form a branch.

One-Woman Campaign

Suzanne was so encouraged that she decided to continue her one-woman campaign.

The circus was being held on a common which was owned by the council. She wrote a letter to the council, asking it to ban the use of animals in the circus.

In its reply, the council said that a contract had already been made with the circus, and it had no power to alter it now, even if it wished to do so.

Suzanne was determined not to be put off. She sent a circular letter to all the local people who had contacted her, telling them what had happened. She invited them to a meeting at her home to discuss what further action they could take.

Nineteen people came to the meeting. They decided to write to the circus owners asking them not to use performing animals. If they refused, they threatened to organise a massive protest campaign.

Circus Options

When the circus owners received the letter, they discussed all the actions they might take. They decided their options were:

▸ to ignore the letter

▸ to reply, stating why they thought there was no harm in using animals

▸ to write a letter to the local paper, explaining their point of view

▸ to invite representatives of the protesters to visit the circus to see how well the animals were treated

▸ to ask for police protection

▸ to employ a security firm to keep the protesters away from the common

▸ to withdraw all the animal acts, apart from the horses

▸ to take out all the animal acts

▸ to cancel the visit altogether.

ACTIVITIES

Questions
1 Which option — or mix of options — would you advise the circus owners to choose? Explain your reasons.

2 Describe the kind of protest campaign Suzanne and her fellow protesters might have organised.

Letter
Write a letter from the circus owners to a local paper, explaining their point of view.

Discussion
How effective have pressure groups been in their campaigns for healthier and safer food?

Change of Structure

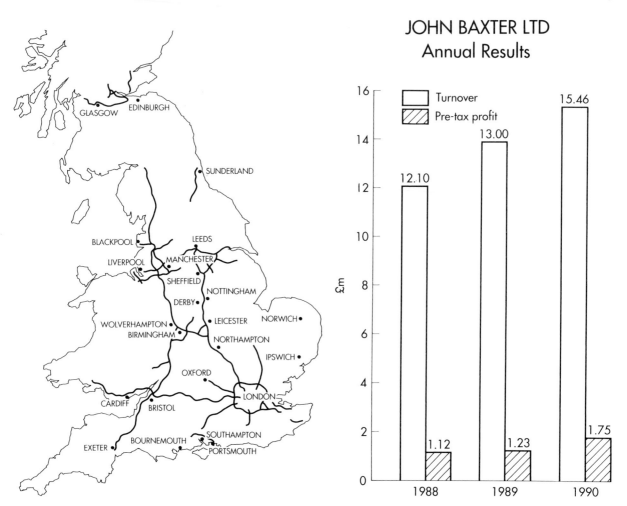

JOHN BAXTER LTD
Annual Results

Two years ago, John Baxter Ltd, a Nottingham foam packaging manufacturer, bought two smaller firms in the same line of business. One factory was in Exeter and the other was in Sunderland.

Although there were some joint activities in the purchase of raw materials, finance, the selection of top managers and research and development, each factory continued to operate independently of the others.

The takeovers were not as successful as the board of directors had expected. In 1990, John Baxter Ltd decided to close the other two firms. After it had paid for the costs of closure, it made £500,000 from selling the factories, the plant and the equipment.

New Organisation

Most of the money was used to extend the Nottingham factory so that production could be increased. At the same time, the structure of the marketing and sales department was changed.

A new Marketing Director was appointed to run the department. Three managers were directly responsible to him – the Export Sales, the Home Sales and the Sales Office Managers.

Britain was divided into eight sales regions, with a Regional Sales Manager in charge of each. In six of the regions, there were a team of four salesmen, led by a team leader. In the other two regions, there were two teams of four, each with its own leader.

ACTIVITIES

Questions
1 What kind of takeovers are described in the case study?

2 Describe the main benefit the firm might have expected to obtain from the takeovers.

3 In your view, what would have been the main cost involved in closing the factories?

4 What percentage net profit did John Baxter Ltd make in each of the three years from 1988 to 1990?

5 What was the reason for the increase in percentage net profit in 1990?

6 In the restructured marketing department, what was the span of control of the Marketing Director and the Home Sales Manager?

7 Draw an organisation chart to show the structure of the new Marketing Department.

8 From a distribution viewpoint, what are the main benefits of Nottingham compared with Exeter and Sunderland?

9 In your view was John Baxter Ltd wise to take the actions that it did? Explain your reasons in full.

Housebuilder's Problems

THE CHILTERN HOME

FOUR EXCLUSIVE NON-ESTATE DETACHED HOUSES OVERLOOKING GOLF COURSE

Set on the outskirts of a charming village, these new executive-style homes are built to the highest standards. Chiltern houses have many impressive features including:

- Four bedrooms and two large reception rooms
- Luxury fitted kitchen with oven, hob and hood, microwave, fridge, and dishwasher
- *En suite* shower and WC in master bedroom
- Luxury family bathroom
- Utility room with freezer, washing machine and tumble drier
- Landscaped garden with patio and barbecue area
- Double garage
- Gas central heating and extra-high insulation throughout
- Full double glazing

Price: £199,500

A medium-sized firm specialises in building executive homes on small, in-fill sites within commuting distance of major cities. It builds two kinds of houses – the four-bedroom Chiltern, and the three-bedroom Stroud (with fewer luxury features), which sells for £165,000.

The firm was one of the first to see that the housing boom might not go on for ever. In 1988, it decided to cut the number of Chiltern houses it built to 235 and increase the output of cheaper Stroud houses to 200. It sold all the houses. It followed the same policy in 1989, building only 200 Chiltern houses and 315 Stroud houses, with far less successful results. It sold all but 15 of the Stroud houses. However, half of the Chiltern houses remained unsold.

Directors' Meeting

A special meeting of the board of directors was called to decide how they might sell the Chiltern houses. They came up with three sales promotion schemes.
Scheme 1 To reduce the price of the houses by £9,500 so that they cost £190,000.
Scheme 2 To reduce the price of the houses by 5 per cent.
Scheme 3 To give buyers £400 a month off their mortgage in the first year; £300 a month in the second year; and £200 a month in the third year.

HOUSES BUILT

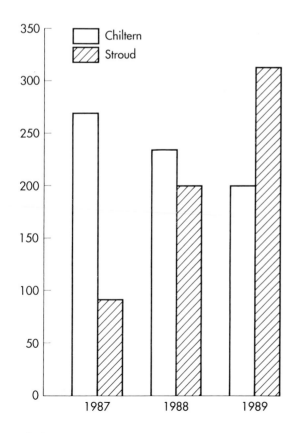

ACTIVITIES

Questions

1 What was the firm's turnover in 1988 and 1989?

2 By what percentage was the turnover reduced in 1989 compared with the previous year?

3 What is the cost of each of the three sales promotion schemes?

4 Which scheme would you advise the firm to adopt? Explain your reasons.

5 Write an advertisement using the same number of words as the one in the case study, giving details about the Chiltern houses and the sales promotion scheme you have chosen.

*S*uperstore

Easyprice National Statistics

Total number of stores	200
Under 20,000 square feet (%)	65
Over 20,000 square feet (%)	35
Average number of employees per 10,000 square feet	70
Full-time employees (%)	30
Part-time employees (%)	70
Weekly sales per square foot (£)	15.25
Net profit margin (%)	6.5

Easyprice, a national chain of supermarkets, is gradually getting rid of its smaller stores and replacing them with larger superstores. In line with this policy, it has decided to close an old, 15,000-square-feet supermarket in a suburban high street, and build a new 35,000-square-feet superstore two miles away, nearer the city centre.

The new superstore will provide one-stop shopping for a vast range of food and household necessities and luxuries. It will have its own in-store bakery, wet-fish and counter-service butchery departments. In addition, there will be a coffee shop, a newspaper and magazine shop, a floral department, and a free community information notice board for local organisations and individuals. There will be car parking for 600 vehicles and a filling station offering discounted petrol and diesel fuel.

*S*ite *P*urchased

Easyprice has already bought the site – a former railway siding – for the superstore. It has now applied to the borough council for planning permission. In support of its application, Easyprice claims that the new development will provide

▶ more local employment
▶ a wider range of goods for a greater number of consumers

- off-street car parking
- easier access for lorries delivering goods
- a community service for local organisations and individuals.

Unhappy Traders

The small shopkeepers in the suburban high street are not at all happy about the closure of the supermarket. They believe that it will greatly reduce the number of shoppers in the high street and, therefore, cut their own trade. Even the two remaining, up-market grocery shops think they will be adversely affected, as the new superstore will be able to sell luxury items at lower prices because of the big discounts Easyprice receives for bulk buying.

One of the traders who will be worst affected is the owner of a corner filling station who relies greatly on selling diesel fuel to taxis at a small discount. Conversations with his taxi-driver customers have convinced him that most of them would buy their fuel at the superstore if it offered bigger discounts, which it almost certainly would.

He estimates that he would lose 40 per cent of his sales. He decides to find out how other traders think they would be affected. The results of his survey were:

Forecast Loss of Sales	%
Fishmonger	45
Filling station	40
Chemists	33
Bakers	28
Florists	23
Ironmonger	22
Kitchen shop	20
Grocers	17
Newsagents	15
Greengrocers	13
Cafés	12
Butchers	10
Stationers	8

Opposition Meeting

The owner of the filling station decides to call a meeting of high-street traders so that they can protest to the council about the Easyprice plan. As a result of their meeting, they send a letter of protest to the borough council. They claim that closing the supermarket would

- destroy the high street as a shopping centre
- create very few local full-time jobs, which might be offset by the need to reduce the number of assistants in their own shops
- create great traffic congestion around the proposed superstore
- make it much more difficult for local senior citizens to shop in a supermarket as they would have to make a long bus journey.

Permission Granted

Despite their protests, planning permission for the new superstore was granted. The traders decided they would carry on their fight. They organised a petition among their customers asking a rival supermarket chain, which specialised in selling basic foods at cut prices in smaller stores, to take over the high-street supermarket.

ACTIVITIES

Questions

Assuming that the new superstore followed the Easyprice national average,

1 How many people would it employ?

2 How many would be

    (a) full-time employees

    (b) part-time employees?

3 What would be the annual turnover of the new superstore?

4 What would its net pretax profit be in £s?

5 What other actions could the high-street traders have taken to oppose the opening of the superstore?

6 Write a local newspaper advertisement for Easyprice explaining the benefits of the new superstore.

7 Do you think the council was right to give planning permission for the new store? Explain your reasons.

8 What are the social costs and benefits of the superstore?

Recruiting Future Managers

GRADUATES IN ALL SUBJECTS		
Where the new degree-winners went:	1988	% of total
Total gaining bachelor's degrees	116,757	100.0
Whereabouts unknown at December 31	14,272	12.2
Returned or moved overseas	8,026	6.9
Further academic study in UK	8,740	7.5
Teacher-training	3,950	3.4
Other training	7,815	6.7
Administrative and managerial work	5,630	4.8
Research, design and development	9,154	7.8
Engineering and science support work	1,236	1.1
Environmental planning	3,377	2.9
Buying, marketing and selling	5,261	4.5
Management services	4,476	3.8
Financial work	9,332	8.0
Information, library and legal work	1,438	1.2
Personnel and welfare services	9,531	8.2
Teaching and lecturing	5,821	5.0
Other kinds of work	4,628	4.0
At best short-term UK job at 31 Dec	14,070	12.0

To recruit its managers of the future, an engineering company had always relied on advertising in university magazines and national newspapers, and on supplying glossy pamphlets and brochures to careers officers and advisers. It also sent out speakers to talk to groups of students.

The results of this recruitment policy were always rather uneven. In some years, the recruitment target was exceeded, but, in others, there was a shortfall. In all years, there were more unsuitable than suitable applicants.

A video about the company was added to the recruitment package, but it had little effect.

Changed System

The company's Personnel Manager was one of the first to realise that the decline in the number of young people would make recruiting students even more difficult in the 1990s. Five years ago, he persuaded the company to introduce a completely new recruiting system.

There would be a two-pronged approach. Under **Plan One**, top A-level students from selected schools and colleges in the area were invited to join the company as management trainees. For a year, they worked in different departments of the company: administration, finance, marketing, sales, production control, production engineering, and research and development.

At the end of the year, suitable trainees were offered employment with the company. They were allowed to choose the department in which they would like to work, subject to the departmental head's approval.

All of them were given time off for study, and the best trainees were given company grants to continue their education full-time at universities or polytechnics.

Plan Two

Under **Plan Two**, university and polytechnic students were invited to work as trainees for a minimum of six weeks during the summer vacation. They were paid a wage of £150 a week.

After four weeks, they were given the chance to move to another department for the rest of their stint, if they wished.

Selected trainees were offered a job with the company, subject to their obtaining at least a second-class honours degree.

Different Approach

The recruiting material was also changed. The glossy pamphlets, full of information about the company, were replaced by word-processed brochures, which gave much more down-to-earth information about the work itself, the challenges involved, and the kinds of skills that were needed. This was supplemented during the training period by seminars conducted by experienced managers.

The new system was more effective than the old, but there was a big difference between the number of trainees who eventually became permanent employees under the two plans.

	Plan One		Plan Two	
Year	Trainees	Employed	Trainees	Employed
1986	3	2	4	1
1987	5	5	3	2
1988	8	8	10	5
1989	9	8	15	4
1990	8	6	18	6

There was also another difference between the two kinds of trainees. Most of the Plan One trainees had studied science or technical subjects at school or college. Plan Two trainees, however, were split 50–50 between those studying the arts and law and those studying science and engineering.

ACTIVITIES

Questions

1 Why would it be more difficult to recruit young people in the 1990s?

2 During the five-year period, what percentages of trainees were taken on as employees under Plan One and Plan Two?

3 In your view, what is the likely reason for the difference?

4 How would you change the recruitment system so that there was less of a difference?

5 Make out a year's training programme for a Plan One trainee, including all the training methods that you think should be included. Explain why you have included them.

A New Venture

Thompson's Cider Profit and Loss Account

	1990	1989
	£000s	
Sales	10,000	9,000
Cost of sales	8,490	7,695
Gross profit	1,510	1,305
Administrative expenses	210	180
Net profit	1,300	1,125
Tax	455	394
Profit after tax	845	731
Dividends	281	210
Profits retained	564	521

Thompson's Cider, an up-market manufacturer, has had another good year, even though sales in the cider market as a whole are falling.

For the last six months, its factory has been working overtime to keep up with demand. Forecast sales for the coming year are even higher, so that it is building an extension to the factory at a cost of £500,000.

The extension will increase the productive capacity by 50 per cent. Not all of this will be needed immediately, so the firm is considering whether it should use the unwanted capacity to produce another kind of up-market drink – pure apple juice. Although there are already many different kinds of non-alcoholic apple drinks on the market, Thompson's Cider believes it can produce a better product than its rivals. It is also confident that the market for non-alcoholic drinks will grow, because of the current concerns about purity of food, slimming, health and the dangers of alcohol – particularly among young ABC1 women.

Market Research

It has commissioned a market-research firm to carry out a survey. The results are most encouraging and confirm many of its own feelings about the market.

The answers to some of the key questions were:

APPLE DRINKS
Report of a Usage and Attitude Survey

All results are expressed as a percentage

Question

'How often do you buy any kind of non-alcoholic apple drink?'

Every day	25
Every week	30
Occasionally	35
Never	10

Question

'Do you buy apple drinks more or less often than you did six months ago?'

	More often	Less often	Don't know
Total	50	20	30
Men	20	30	50
Women	80	10	10

Question

'Did you find the last brand of apple drink you bought satisfactory or unsatisfactory?'

	Satisfactory	Unsatisfactory
ABC1	40	60
C2DE	70	30

Tasting Panel

The firm made some samples of the drink it planned to produce and asked a tasting panel of men, women and children to sample it. The results were again very encouraging, as it scored highly with all three groups.
Some of the comments were of great interest, too.

'It's not too fizzy'
Girl, ten years of age, social group B
'I'd drink this instead of wine every time'
Woman, 29, A
'Like a champagne cider – without the hangover'
Man, 55, A
'Just the stuff you can drink with the kids'
Man, 34, C2

Forecast Budget

The firm was so encouraged that it got a production and financial team to work out a budget for the first year. The forecast profit and loss account was:

	£
Sales	800,000
Cost of sales	624,000
Gross profit	176,000
Administrative expenses	16,000
Net profit	160,000

However, there were still many other matters to discuss, such as the name of the drink and the form of packaging, before the firm decided to go ahead.

ACTIVITIES

Questions

1 State three items which would form part of the 'cost of sales' in a profit and loss account.

2 What was the percentage increase in the turnover of Thompson's Cider in 1990 compared with the previous year?

3 What was the net-profit margin in 1989 and 1990?

4 What was the forecast net-profit margin for the new apple drink?

5 In what ways could the firm finance the building of its factory extension? Which method would you advise it to use in this case? Explain your reasons.

6 Write the first ten questions of a market-research questionnaire for a usage and attitude survey about apple drinks.

7 What name would you advise the firm to use for its new drink? State your reasons.

8 In your view, how should the drink be packaged? Include a sketch in your answer.

9 Using all the information in the case study, write a report recommending whether the firm should produce the new drink or not.

A Bank Manager's Decision

Balance Sheet

	31 December Current year £000	31 December Previous year £000
Fixed assets		
Land and buildings	2,000	1,750
Plant and machinery	3,000	2,750
	5,000	4,500
Current assets		
Stock	8,000	5,000
Debtors	17,500	8,500
Cash	500	3,000
	26,000	16,500
Current liabilities		
Creditors	13,000	7,500
Overdraft	10,000	4,000
	23,000	11,500
Net current assets	3,000	5,000
Total assets, less current liabilities	8,000	9,500
Creditors, amounts falling due after one year	2,000	2,500
Net assets	6,000	7,000
Represented by:		
Share capital	8,000	5,500
Reserves	(2,000)	1,500
	6,000	7,000

A furniture manufacturing firm has asked its bank manager to increase its present overdraft of £10 million to £15 million. In support of its request, it has provided a cash-flow forecast, its latest balance sheet for the current and the previous year, and other financial documents.

The bank manager takes a look at the cash-flow forecast and then glances through the balance sheet, which is set out in the modern, single-column form. The balance sheet enables her to come to a quick decision.

ACTIVITIES

1 Give one example of:

   (a) a fixed asset

   (b) a current asset

   (c) an intangible asset.

2 What is the main importance of an overdraft for businesses?

3 By how much has the firm's overdraft increased during the year?

4 What is the firm's current working capital? By what percentage has it increased or decreased compared with the previous year?

5 Using the acid test ratio, state whether the firm is more or less solvent than it was in the previous year. Show your calculations.

6 Apart from increasing its overdraft, what other means has the firm used to finance its operations during the current year?

7 Suggest reasons why the furniture manufacturing firm may have run into financial difficulties.

8 If you were the bank manager, would you agree to increase the overdraft or not? Explain your reasons.

9 Shortly after the bank manager came to her decision, many of the big stores, which were the firm's main customers, announced that they were giving interest-free credit for two years on furniture. How might that have affected:

   (a) the manufacturing firm

   (b) the bank manager's decision?

Grant's Gallery

Terry Grant had never been much of a businessman. If he had, he would never have become an actor!

At drama school, he had dreamt of being a megastar, but reality was quite different. He spent most of his life waiting for the telephone to ring, but it rarely did.

He got a few small parts on television; some engagements at London fringe theatres; and a greater number with companies touring from one provincial city to another. Christmas was the only bright spot in the year. He always got a part in a pantomime at a theatre on the south coast – for a whole month.

Big Break

Then, one day, his big break seemed to have come. He went for an audition as the male lead in a new play and got the part. Three months later, after a try-out tour, the play opened in the West End. His name – TERRY GRANT – glowed in lights above the crowded streets of London's theatreland.

The play got good reviews, and so did he. For the first time in his life, he had some real money to spend. Although he bought himself a few luxuries, he didn't waste his money. He had a feeling that his luck might not last.

The play ran for six months before it folded. His name was replaced by another actor's name above the theatre. He went back to waiting by the silent telephone again.

The Decision

Terry decided that he had had enough of acting. He went down to the south coast for a few days to think about what he could do instead.

As he was wandering round the seaside town, he happened to glance in an estate agent's window. The lease of a small shop, with a flat above, was being offered at a remarkably low price. The rent was cheap, too. It gave him the idea he had been waiting for.

In his whole life, he had only ever done one clever thing from a business viewpoint.

As an actor, he had been unemployed – or 'resting' as theatrical people call it – for most of the time. To make some money, he had started buying watercolour paintings, which at that time could be picked up very cheaply for £10 or £20, or even less. He took a stall in Portobello market, and sold some of the paintings at a good profit, which helped him to survive while he was 'resting'.

However, watercolours were not so popular then as they were later. As a result, he accumulated a large number of watercolours, whose value went on rising year by year.

Art Gallery

'Why don't I open an art gallery?' he asked himself.

With the money he had made in the West End, the sale of a few watercolours, and the help of a bank manager, he bought the lease of the shop. His name was once again above the streets – though not in lights – as he called his business GRANT'S GALLERY.

A few months after he opened the gallery, Terry showed that he could be a businessman – if he tried hard enough. With his actor's charm, he persuaded the managers of some of the best hotels in town to display one of his watercolours in their lobby with a small poster advertising the gallery beside it.

His enterprise paid off. His best customers were wealthy, young London couples on weekend breaks who wanted to take back a souvenir of their visit. He also acquired a few local customers, including one middle-aged lady who remembered seeing him in the West End play.

He replenished his declining stock of watercolours at local sales, though he often found it difficult to compete with the bids of other dealers.

The gallery didn't make him a fortune – just enough to live on. However, he was quite happy.

The Crisis

Then, he had a couple of shocks, which made him feel really desperate. He had completely forgotten that the lease of his premises included a rent review every five years. When he opened the letter from the owner's solicitors, he found that the rent had doubled.

A few days later, he got another letter informing him of the new business rates for the year. They were almost double, too.

He didn't know what to do. It was obvious that he would have to make some big changes.

That weekend, an old chum from his acting days, who had become a highly successful theatrical agent, came down for a visit. Terry told his friend about his problems.

His friend thought for a moment. 'Why don't you go into picture framing? That would bring in some extra revenue. Or you could go really down market by selling cheap little framed prints of local views, and opening up the courtyard at the back as a tearoom.'

Terry decided to investigate his chum's ideas.

Framing Franchise

First of all, he found out about framing franchises.

If Fast Frame accepted him as a franchisee, he would have to move to a different shop in the high street which they selected.

The total cost of the franchise was £49,000; but up to two-thirds of this amount could be borrowed from the bank. The minimum capital required, therefore, was £16,000.

Terry did not have that amount of money. He would have to sell his present shop, if he could, and buy a flat to live in. 'Or', he thought, 'I might be able to let the shop and go on living in the flat above.'

expert picture framing

TYPICAL RESULTS FOR FIRST THREE YEARS

	Year 1	Year 2	Year 3
Turnover (Net Vat)	£85,000	£105,000	£120,000
Management Fee (6¼%)	5,312	6,562	7,500
Marketing Services Fee (6¼%)	5,312	6,562	7,500
Cost of Sales (Materials)	19,125	23,625	27,000
Credit Card Charges	595	735	840
Gross Profit	**£54,655**	**£67,515**	**£77,160**
Wages & N.H.I.	9,310	14,980	16,478
Rent, Rates & Insurance	21,250	22,250	23,000
Gas, Water & Electricity	1,200	1,260	1,323
Postage, Stationery & Telephone	1,200	1,260	1,323
Accountancy	500	1,000	1,200
Sundry	1,200	1,500	1,800
Net Profit (before Depreciation and Interest. Drawings and Tax)	**£19,995**	**£25,265**	**£32,036**
	(23.52%)	(24.06%)	(26.69%)

IMPORTANT NOTES:

1. The above estimates are based on existing operating shops. They are intended for guidance only and should not be interpreted as a guarantee that any specific franchise will make a profit. Adjustments may be required according to location.

2. Up to ⅔rds finance of the total capital requirement can be funded through National Westminster and Barclays Franchise Finance schemes e.g. £10,000 borrowed over 5 years costs approx. £230.00 per month repayment. This should be taken into consideration when calculating potential returns.

3. Wages: those franchisees who operate husband and wife teams may reduce costs accordingly.

4. The above assumes no review of rent level.

FRANCHISE OF THE YEAR

10.88

Own Business

He then found out about running his own framing business at the gallery. The local college ran a week's course in picture framing. He made an appointment to see the lecturer in charge.

She told him that the equipment would cost about £9,000. Terry thought his bank manager would give him a loan.

The lecturer also said that, once he was skilled, he should be able to frame three average-sized prints or photographs in an hour. These would sell for £25 each. The cost of the materials was one-third.

Terry felt sure that the course would provide him with all the knowledge and skills he needed.

One advantage of this scheme was that it would add very little to his overheads. The main expense would be the repayment of the bank loan for the equipment. At current interest rates, this would be £200 a month over five years.

Tea Room

Terry then started thinking about the third idea. He decided that he could easily convert the storeroom and the courtyard at the back of the shop into a tearoom with the help of some of his local friends. He could pay for the materials out of his current earnings, as they wouldn't cost him very much. The cost of hiring equipment and some furniture would be £2,500 a year. He would have to employ part-time workers in the tearoom. The annual wage bill would be £4,000, as the tearoom would not remain open the whole year. The net profit on the teas and snacks would be 40 per cent. He already knew an artist in the town who could produce small sketches of local views at £10 each, which would retail at £15.

ACTIVITIES

Questions

1 If Terry took out a Fast Frame franchise, by what percentage could he expect his turnover to increase in the second year and in the third year?

2 Why do the costs of sales increase as turnover rises?

3 If a franchisee took out a £10,000 bank loan, what effect would it have on the net profits in the first year? Show your calculations.

4 If Terry set up his own picture-framing business, what would be the break-even point? Illustrate your answer with a chart.

5 What are the main points which would be included in a local paper advertisement to recruit part-time staff for the tearoom?

6 Which of the three options would you advise Terry to choose? Explain your reasons in full.

7 Draw up a business plan for the option you have chosen which could be sent to a bank manager with a request for finance. You should use the following headings:

▶ Aims
▶ Objectives
▶ Markets
▶ Financial analysis and prospects.

8 Do you think Terry was wise to give up his career as an actor and open an art gallery in a seaside town? What other options did he have then?

Mobile Telephones

C A S E · S T U D Y · F O R T Y · T H R E E

Mobile (or cellular) telephones have been one of the growth markets of the late 1980s. They allow business persons to keep in permanent contact with the outside world by using in-car radio phones or portable radio telephones.

Britain was one of the first European countries to take advantage of this revolution in communications, and now has 56 per cent of the radio telephone users in the European Community. The radio links are provided by two main networks. To meet the demand for mobile phones, dozens of car-phone firms have been started in all parts of the country. They sell, lease or hire the necessary equipment and install the phones in cars. Subscribers pay a one-off connection fee, a monthly charge and up to 38p a minute for inland calls.

Mobile Telephones in Europe

End Year	Subscribers	Cost (car unit) (£)
1985	49,000	1,420
1986	122,000	1,290
1987	260,000	1,200
1988	498,000	731
1989	578,000 (April)	354 (May)

Source: European Mobile Communications Research

Market Entry

Gayland Rentals plc was one of the first firms to set up a car-phone company in London in 1985. As its core, or main, business is renting television sets, it already had a large staff of electronic engineers, and long experience of renting out and installing equipment.

For the first three years, the firm concentrated on building up a secure subscriber base in London. However, for the last two years, it has expanded its car-phone business in other parts of the country by buying up smaller car-phone firms.

In 1988, it bought two car-phone companies. In 1989, it spent £18 million on acquiring three more companies.

GAYLAND RENTALS plc
ANNUAL REPORT AND ACCOUNTS, 1990

CHAIRMAN'S REPORT

Despite the great increase in trading difficulties, I am happy to report that the company had one of its best years in 1989. Turnover rose from £28 million in 1988 to £60 million in 1989. Profits before tax also showed a very satisfactory increase of 50 per cent, from £2 million in 1988 to £3 million in 1989.

TELEVISION RENTALS
Our core business continued to make substantial progress in 1989, though at a somewhat lower rate than in recent

---

years. Owing to the squeeze on consumer spending, the growth in the satellite-television market was not as great as anticipated. However, as interest rates fall, demand can be expected to rise. Your company is ready to take full advantage of any upsurge in demand.

MOBILE TELEPHONES

The company's decision to enter the mobile-telephone market at an early stage has been fully justified by the results. Once the London base had been consolidated, the board of directors decided to expand operations to other areas to increase the company's market share.

This policy has been an enormous success, which is reflected in the great increase in turnover and profits before tax.

The company will continue its policy of expansion during the coming year by buying further car-phone companies in the provinces.

Although estimates of a total market of 15 million subscribers for cellular phones may be exaggerated, there is still an enormous potential for expansion before saturation point is reached.

RESULTS AT A GLANCE

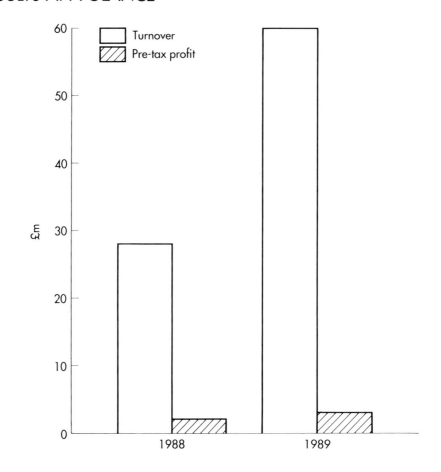

Balance Sheet
at 31 December 1989

	31 December 1989 £000	31 December 1988 £000
Fixed assets		
Tangible assets	4,000	3,250
Current assets		
Stock	7,000	6,500
Debtors	15,500	7,500
Cash	500	1,000
	23,000	15,000
Creditors, amounts falling due within one year	20,000	6,000
Net current assets	3,000	9,000
Total assets, less current liabilities	7,000	12,500
Creditors, amounts falling due after one year	3,000	4,250
	4,000	8,000
Represented by:		
Share capital	3,900	3,900
Reserves	100	4,100
	4,000	8,000

ACTIVITIES

Questions

1 What are the main advantages of radio telephones for business persons?

2 By what percentage did the market for mobile telephones increase in Europe between 1985 and 1988?

3 How many people in Britain were radio-telephone users in April 1989?

4 What kind of takeovers have been made by Gayland Rentals plc?

5 By what percentage did the company's turnover increase in 1989? What, in your view, was mainly responsible for the rise?

6 What was the company's working capital in 1989?

7 Use ratios to find out if the company might have any problems with working capital. Show your workings.

8 Using all the information in the case study, state whether you think the company was wise to expand its cellular-phone operations in the way it did. Explain your reasons in full, and describe any alternative strategies it could have adopted.

Mr Fish!

Steve King loved fishing, which was just as well as there was very little for young people to do in the village where he lived. There wasn't much more to do in the nearest town of Stanton.

Stanton and district had very little industry. It was mainly a retirement area for wealthy people from other parts of the country, who lived in the little villages between the pretty town of Duncton, with its Catholic boarding school, and the coast.

From the age of 13, Steve used to go fishing in the River Darwent most summer evenings and practically every weekend. He became so keen that he often used to sneak off for a quiet day's fishing, which didn't help his GCSE results at all. Steve had made no plans for a career. He would have liked to work on a trawler, but the fishing fleet at Portside had declined ever since the shoals of mackerel had moved away. The few remaining boats could scarcely net a living for their skippers.

When Steve left school at 16, he was lucky to get a job as a junior storeman at the shoe factory in Stanton, which was the main employer in the area. The firm was expanding as it had just taken over a shoe-manufacturing firm in Germany.

The Crisis

Steve had been working at the factory for three years, when his whole life changed.

First, he met Emma, an 18-year-old business studies student, at a party. They took to each other straight away and started seeing each other regularly. Fishing dropped into the background – for a time!

Then, three months later, he lost his job. His firm had decided to make all its shoes in Germany.

Steve tried to get another job, but without success. To fill in time, he started fishing on the river again.

One day, as he was glancing through an old newspaper, an advertisement caught his eye. It gave him a great idea. He could scarcely wait to discuss it with Emma that night.

Steve's Idea

MOBILE FISH VAN Profitable one-person business in Yorkshire. Turnover £70,000 a year. Net profit, £15,400. Good area. Scope for improvement. £17,500.

'Look at this, Emma,' Steve said excitedly, handing her the newspaper cutting. As Emma read the advertisement, her face dropped.

'Yorkshire's miles away!'

'Oh, I wasn't thinking of moving. It just gave me an idea. I could start my own mobile fish shop here. I worked it all out today. I could buy the fish from the wholesaler in Portside . . .'

'Don't forget the trout farm . . .'

'Oh, yes, I hadn't thought of that. I could sell fish in Enford on Tuesday, in Duncton on Friday and in Stanton on Saturday. On Wednesday and Thursday, I could go around the villages. I could easily buy some sort of van from my redundancy money.'

'What about Sunday and Monday?' Emma asked, laughing.

'I might go fishing – when I wasn't seeing you! Do you think it would work, Emma?'

Emma pursed her lips. After a pause, she said: 'It could, Steve. There are a lot of rich old people around here who might like having fish delivered to their door. It depends on how well you advertise the service. But, we'll have to get some facts and figures first.'

They decided to share the research between them. Steve agreed to find out about costs and prices, while Emma would do some general research about the market and advertising.

The Market

Emma was the first to come up with some figures.

National Expenditure of One-Adult Households

Retired households mainly dependent on state pensions			Other retired households		
Gross weekly income					
Under £45	£45 and under £60	£60 or more	Under £80	£80 and under £125	£125 or more
44%	36%	20%	36%	36%	28%
Expenditure on food					
£12.90	£13.45	£15.42	£12.83	£16.18	£17.91

Source: Department of Employment, Family Expenditure Survey 1986 (adapted)

Stanton and District Expenditure of One-Adult Households

Retired households mainly dependent on state pensions			Other retired households		
Gross weekly income					
Under £45	£45 and under £60	£60 or more	Under £80	£80 and under £125	£125 or more
49%	33%	18%	27%	38%	35%
Expenditure on food					
£12.40	£13.10	£14.29	£15.10	£17.82	£19.33

She had also obtained some general information about the market. In the last 20 years, the market for fresh fish had declined. There were now only 2,500 wet-fish shops in the country.

The main reasons for the decline were:

▶ difficulties in cooking fresh fish

▶ the increased use of convenience foods, such as frozen fish fingers and breaded scampi

▶ fewer Catholics eating fish on Fridays

▶ poor marketing.

However, many older people still liked to eat fresh fish.

Market Growth

Recently, however, the size of the market had started to increase. The main reasons were:

- slimmers like to eat baked or steamed white fish because it was high in protein and low in carbohydrates

- many people had become vegetarians, but some of them continued to eat fish as a replacement for meat

- improved marketing and publicity.

As a result, some supermarkets now had fresh-fish counters. However, none of the supermarkets in Stanton and district had a fresh-fish section yet.

There was one small wet-fish shop in Portside; and one of the greengrocers in Duncton also sold fish, though most of it was frozen.

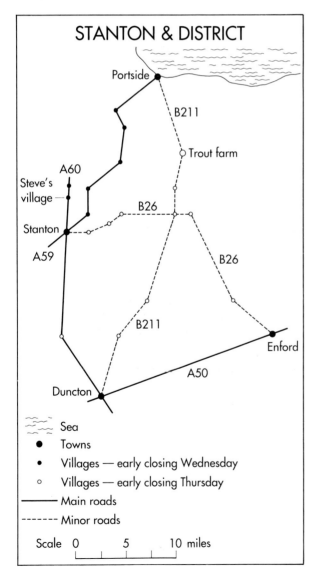

Costs

Steve had made some estimates of how much it would cost to run the business per year.

	£
Road Tax	100
Insurance	400
Repairs and servicing	500
Petrol	1,750
Depreciation	250
Advertising	1,000

He had also calculated that the average cost of the fish he bought would be £1.50 per lb.

Emma checked the figures and studied the route map Steve had made for his weekly trips.

'Wouldn't it be better to visit villages with the same early-closing day on Wednesdays and Thursdays, Steve? People wouldn't have the chance to pop into their village shop after one o'clock, so they might be more inclined to buy from you. You could save on petrol, too, if you made nice round trips.'

Advertising

Emma had also obtained some information about the costs of advertising.

Commercial Radio

Easy Listening, which is the local commercial station for Stanton and district, covers the whole of the county and parts of two other counties.

The prime-time segment, from 7 am to 11 am, has the biggest audience of ABC1 housewives. A ten-second spot advertisement in prime time costs £150.

Local Newspaper

The *Stanton & District Gazette* has a total circulation of 30,000, of which 60 per cent is delivered to the door. The cost per single-column centimetre for display advertisements is £20.

Steve and Emma both thought that the minimum size should be a double-column advertisement 5 centimetres deep, which would cost £200.

Circulars

Emma's uncle, who owns a printing firm, has offered to print circulars for £5 per thousand.

The cost of door-to-door drops is £15 per 1,000.

The total number of houses in the target villages is 5,000.

An Unexpected Offer

Steve and Emma were about to find out some more facts and figures, when Emma's uncle offered Steve a job as a sales representative in his printing firm.

'It's very tempting', said Steve, 'but I think I'd rather try to make it on my own. I happened to see a poster about the Enterprise Allowance Scheme today. If you've been unemployed for eight weeks and can invest £1,000 in your business, the government will pay you £40 a week for a year. That will be a big help.'

ACTIVITIES

Questions

1 Give one example from the case study of the three sectors of production — primary, secondary, tertiary.

2 Why might the shoe manufacturer have decided to move production to Germany?

3 Steve adopted Emma's suggestion that on Wednesdays and Thursdays he should visit as many villages with the same early-closing day as possible. Make out a chart, including the road numbers, showing the most economical routes for those two days. What is the approximate mileage per day? (Remember that he has to go to Portside and the trout farm each day to collect supplies.)

4 In Steve's estimates of his costs, which are:

(a) fixed costs

(b) variable costs?

How much are the total estimated costs per year?

5 If the average price of the fish he sold was £2.30 per lb, what would be the break-even point? Illustrate your answer with a chart.

6 What would be the best way for Steve to advertise his business? Make out an advertising budget for the first year, showing the kind of advertisement, the month in which it should be used, and the cost. (Your budget must not exceed £1,000.)

7 Use the market-research information in the case study to state whether you think Steve's business is likely to succeed. Explain your reasons in full.

8 Emma's uncle had offered Steve a salary of £6,000, a company car, and 2½ per cent commission on sales. During his first year, Steve's sales should total £100,000. If you were Steve, would you take the job with Emma's uncle or set up in business on your own? Give reasons for your choice.

Go West!

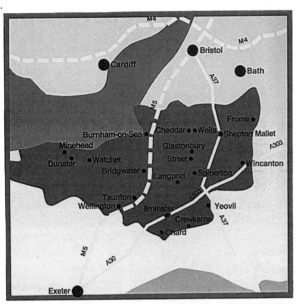

Labour supply – flexible, hard-working with excellent industrial relations.

Perhaps the most important benefit for companies moving into the county has been their new workforce. The working population is expected to be 224,000 by 1991 – and in many areas there is a considerable reserve of female and part-time labour.

Wage rates tend to be lower than the average for the rest of the country, and significantly lower than for other industrial areas. Yet the labour force is skilled and willing to travel considerable distances to work.

The record of industrial disputes is excellent. There is a complete absence of major disputes – with a lower number of working days lost, and relatively few workers involved in stoppages.

Source: Somerset – The Enterprising Environment (adapted)

A medium-sized firm, which manufactures chemicals, is thinking of moving from its present factory near London to an enterprise zone in the North or to Somerset.

The firm has already arranged a number of free trips for employees and their families to both parts of the country, but the number of employees who took advantage of the offer was smaller than expected.

All employees were then asked to state if they would be willing to move with the firm to the northern enterprise zone or to Somerset. Again, the number of people who replied to the opinion survey was smaller than expected.

The results of the survey, expressed as a percentage, were:

	Senior management	Middle management	Junior management	Supervisors	Manual workers	Office staff
North	70	50	32	25	15	10
West	85	65	25	20	12	15

Final Decision

The Managing Director had called a meeting of his top managers to make a final decision that he could then present to the board of directors.

Marketing Director:
I'm in favour of the West. The M5 runs right through Somerset, and links with the M4 to give access to London. From Bridgwater, a lorry can reach London or Birmingham in three hours.

There are rail freightliner terminals at Bristol and Exeter. That could be useful for our exports when the Channel Tunnel opens in 1993, with its high-speed shuttle service of freight trains to the Continent. And Heathrow is only two or three hours away.

Purchasing Manager:
I agree. The communications are excellent. There are good container ports at Avonmouth and Southampton, not far away; and there are roll on/roll off ferries to the Continent from Plymouth and Poole.

Production Controller:
I'm a little worried that we might lose too many supervisors and key workers. It's strange that more of them are willing to go north.

Personnel Manager:
That's because houses are still cheaper there; but the prices are increasing.

We're going to lose a lot of employees wherever we go, so we'll just have to make up a good package of fringe benefits for essential workers.

I'm sure we'll have no trouble in recruiting the workers we need in Somerset. And there are fewer strikes and stoppages. That certainly appeals to me!

Finance Director:
I think we should move north. I agree that Somerset has many advantages, but just think of all the financial benefits we'd obtain in an enterprise zone. No business rates for ten years; 100 per cent capital allowances for new buildings . . .

Managing Director:
That's right! But they're all one-off benefits. We've got to think of the long term, too. There's nothing more important than a skilled, loyal workforce. In my view, we're more likely to find that in Somerset.

Finance Director:
That's a bit harsh. The workers in the North are just as skilled and loyal as any other workers in the country. They're no trouble if they're working for a progressive company like ours. The Japanese have proved that!

Managing Director:
At the moment, that's true. But it might be different without all the trade-union laws. Say the Labour Party gets into power. If they repeal any of the trade-union laws, it might be a different story.

Personnel Manager:
Don't forget that the wages in Somerset are much lower than in other industrial areas.

Managing Director:
That's an important point, too. I take it the majority agree that we should move to Somerset . . . I'll put that proposal to the board.

ACTIVITIES

Questions
1 Suggest reasons for the big differences in the percentage of senior management and office staff who would be willing to move with the firm.

2 Explain why good communications are important in choosing a new site for a factory.

3 Make up a package of fringe benefits which might persuade

   (a) a person in middle management

   (b) a skilled worker

   to move with a firm.

4 Describe the different kinds of financial aid which government provides for businesses, and explain its importance in deciding to move to a new location.

5 Describe the recent trade-unions laws and explain what effects they have had on

   (a) business

   (b) trade unions.

6 Do you think the Finance Director's views were sensible? Explain your reasons in full.

Night Life

Steve had always had a good eye for business. While he was still at school, he opened his first business – a swap service for computer games on which he made a good commission.

When he left college, he was taken on as a trainee by a big hotel chain. By his mid-twenties, he had become an assistant manager at one of the chain's biggest hotels. While he was there, he met Paula, who was working as an assistant chef. Four months later, they were married.

Own Business

Although they both liked working for the hotel group, they decided that they could have a more exciting life, and make much more money, if they had their own business. There was very little risk involved, as they could always get jobs again in hotels or catering, if their business failed. But they were determined that would not happen.

They bought a run-down guest house from an old couple who were retiring. Within five years they had boosted the turnover from £40,000 to £120,000. There was little chance of expanding the business further, and they both wanted a new challenge. So, they decided to sell the guest house and start a new business. They put it on the market at £375,000 and it was soon snapped up at £350,000, because of its high net profit of 35 per cent.

NightLife
Saturday, 16th July

SUSAN DAVID

Television and screen star
Tickets £12

NightLife
Wednesday, 13th July

ILLUSIONS

Fast-moving dance and song team from the United States
Tickets £4.50

NightLife
Thursday, 21st July

THE BIG BAND

The Glenn Miller Sound
Tickets £12

New Venture

The sale netted them £250,000. Steve and Paula decided to go up market and open a licensed restaurant where they would serve only the best food and quality wines. There would be dancing every night and a floor show twice a week with alternating local, national and foreign entertainers.

They were looking around for an established business to buy, preferably one which was a little run down so they could build it up again as they had done with the guest house.

They were considering three possibilities:

LONDON SUBURB Established restaurant with supper, music, dance and full justices on licence, currently seating 90 in 1,500 square feet. Large unused basement which could seat another 80. Good kitchens. First-class trading position. Turnover split 50–50 between food and wet sales. Current turnover £250,000, but still scope for improvement. Secure 15-year lease. Only £149,000.	**BRIGHTON** Licensed restaurant with music and dancing and full justices on licence. Holiday and residential trade. Over 2,000 square feet. Newly installed kitchens. Three-room flat. Business closed for six months owing to owner's illness. Reduced for quick sale – £200,000 freehold.	**SUPERB LICENSED RESTAURANT AND TEAROOMS** in well-known beauty spot near London. Full justices on music and dancing licences. 120-cover restaurant and adjoining 50-cover tearooms. First-rate fixtures and fittings. Large car park. Takings £9,000 weekly during summer peak. Bungalow in grounds. £350,000 freehold.

After Steve and Paula had visited the restaurants, examined the books and made their own investigations, they decided to buy the restaurant at Brighton.

Refurbishment

They decided that the restaurant had to be totally refurbished, apart from the kitchens and the dance floor which were both new. They employed an architect to create a brand new image, with ceiling lights which gave a view of the night skies; a bar in the shape of the new moon; and intimate alcoves, shaped like space capsules, along one wall.

The old carpet, which was very worn, was ripped out and replaced by a dark-blue carpet. The walls were painted pale blue and decorated with blown-up photographs of the planets.

The old sound system was replaced by the latest quadraphonic disco sound system with new strobe lights and neon decor tubes.

The total cost of the refurbishment was £500,000.

Recruiting Staff

To head the kitchen brigade, they recruited a young English chef who had already made a name for himself in top London hotels. They decided to employ part-time waitresses. Their advertisement in the local evening paper produced many applicants, because they were offering high wages.

They contacted a theatrical agency to obtain a range of entertainers for their shows.

Steve and Paula spent a long time choosing a name for their restaurant. Eventually, after much discussion, they decided to call it NightLife.

Opening Night

The restaurant opened on 1 July. The first night was a resounding success. They had to turn away as many people as the restaurant could seat, but they took the opportunity to book them in for future nights.

In July, they exceeded the forecast monthly sales of £40,000 in their business plan by £2,000.

FORECAST SALES

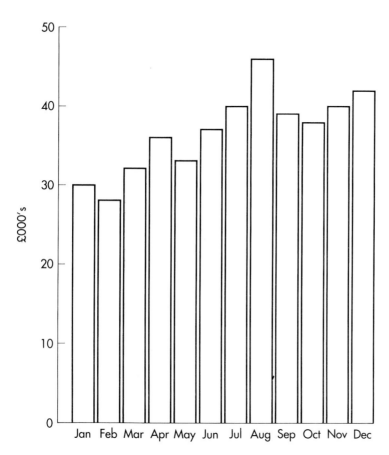

August was not so good. Forecast sales were £46,000; but actual sales were £38,000. The takings in September were even worse. Forecast sales were £39,000; actual sales were only £30,000.

By October, sales had fallen to £25,000.

The Choice

Steve and Paula knew that something had to be done quickly. They spent the whole of the day discussing it, and decided there were only two choices:

(a) They could get rid of the food side of their business and turn the restaurant into a down-market disco.

(b) They could alter the nature of the business entirely by using it as a conventional restaurant, open for morning coffees, lunches, teas and evening meals.

It took them another week to come to a decision.

ACTIVITIES

Questions

1 Why do you think Steve and Paula chose the restaurant at Brighton? Which restaurant would you have chosen to buy?

2 What sources of finance could they have used to refurbish the restaurant? Take one source and explain its main advantages and disadvantages.

3 What kind of image were they trying to create with their refurbished restaurant?

4 In view of what happened in the case study, do you think NightLife was a suitable name for the restaurant? Suggest an alternative and explain why it would have been better.

5 Design an advertisement for the evening paper to recruit part-time waiting staff for NightLife.

6 What was the difference between their total forecast and actual sales for July to September inclusive?

7 Explain the differences between the forecast sales for each month in the chart.

8 Apart from the forecast sales, what other items would Steve and Paula have included in their business plan? Take one of the items and explain its importance.

9 In view of what happened in the case study, do you think they made sufficient investigations before they bought the restaurant? Suggest what other investigations they might have made and explain their importance.

10 Which plan, (a) or (b), should they choose for the future of their business? Explain all your reasons.

Really Bad News!

C A S E · S T U D Y · F O R T Y · S E V E N

Five years ago, one of the directors of Printing & Packaging plc had persuaded the board of directors to start publishing trade and technical magazines.

The new Magazines Division had never done very well; and, over the last two years, its profits had started to fall. During the current year, its profits had fallen even further.

Printing & Packaging plc

Pre-Tax Profits – Divisional Results
(unaudited)

Division	Current year £000	Previous year £000	% + or −
Packaging	2,620	1,360	+ 93
Printing	2,348	2,090	+ 12
Magazines	846	1,262	− 33
	5,814	4,172	+ 39

'The results from the Magazines Division are even worse than I expected,' said Alec, the Managing Director.

'That's right,' said Bill, who was the Finance Director. 'It's really clawed our profits back.' He tapped away at his calculator for a few seconds. 'Without the Magazines Division, our total profits would have been much higher. We'll have to take strong measures.'

'We could try and sell the division to a bigger firm of publishers,' Bianca, the Personnel Manager, suggested.

'With *its* track record, there's not much chance of that,' Bill replied. 'I think we ought to close it down, before it starts to make a loss.'

Redundancies

Alec frowned. 'I wouldn't like to do that. We've ploughed so much money into that division. But there'll have to be some redundancies. Could you work out the details, Bill, before the end of the month? We could include a printed announcement with their pay slips then.'

'That's a bit harsh, isn't it?' said Bianca. 'There's plenty of time to discuss it with the shop stewards first. If we don't, there might be trouble with the other workers.'

'No way!' said Alec, curtly. 'Tell the workers the bad news just before it happens, and let them argue about it afterwards – that's my view.'

'At least, we could do something to soften the blow,' Bianca said. 'How about putting up a poster explaining the reasons for the redundancies?'

'No, we'll do it my way,' said Alec firmly.

Bianca knew that it was useless to argue; but she said to herself that Alec would be in for a shock if the European Commission got its way, and all firms had to have worker–directors on their boards.

ACTIVITIES

Questions
1 Explain the meaning of the following words and phrases in the case study:

   (a) plc

   (b) board of directors

   (c) division

   (d) pre-tax profits

   (e) unaudited

   (f) redundancies

   (g) shop stewards

   (h) worker–directors

2 By what percentage would the firm's pre-tax profits have risen without the magazines division?

3 What details would Bill have had to work out in relation to the redundancies?

4 Write a poster which Bianca might have displayed to explain the reasons for the firm's actions.

5 In your view, which is the best way of dealing with the problem? Explain your reasons in full.

Attracting Women Workers

J F Brown Ltd, a medium-sized engineering firm, has had a very good year. For the third year in succession, it has increased its exports – to a record 70 per cent. As a result, it was one of only 120 firms in the country to receive the Queen's Award for Export on the Queen's birthday in April. This gave it the right to fly the Queen's Award yellow and blue flag from its factory, and to use a symbol, containing the Royal crown, on its letters and packaging.

The firm's salesmen (wearing their smart, new Queen's Award ties) soon found that the Award helped them to win many more orders, particularly in Third World countries. The order books were full for the next two years.

There was only one snag. The increase in orders meant far more paperwork. Unfortunately, there was a great turnover in office staff, with a large proportion leaving every year. It took a long time to train new office workers to handle the complicated export forms.

Ken Rose, the young Managing Director, had called a meeting with the Finance Director and the Personnel Officer to discuss the problem.

Staff Turnover

'You've got some figures for us?' Ken said, turning to Jayne, the Personnel Officer.

'Yes,' she said, handing copies of a typed table to the two men.

Turnover Rate – Office Staff

	Employees leaving	Total staff (excluding temps)	Annual turnover rate (%)
1989	10	52	19
1990	16	57	28
1991	21	60	35

'As you can see, the situation's not improving,' Jayne added. 'The staff turnover rate is over one-third this year, and as far as I can see, it can only get worse. I thought the Queen's Award might help us to keep staff, but it hasn't.'

'What's the basic problem?' asked John, the Finance Director.

'It's a threefold problem,' said Jayne.

'(a) As you both know, there are far fewer young girls – and boys – coming on to the labour market, so it's not easy to obtain young workers.

(b) It's also difficult to get young mothers to go back to work, and

(c) – this is the big one – even when we're lucky enough to get married women to work for us, they often don't stay long, because we just don't compete with all the fringe benefits offered by big firms.'

'I thought we did rather well on that score,' said Ken. 'We provide a good pension scheme, sick and maternity leave, life insurance and a subsidised dining room. And there's no firm, however big, which gives better training than we do.'

'That's part of the problem,' said Jayne. 'No sooner do we train new workers, than they go off to bigger firms which provide many more fringe benefits.'

'So, what's the answer, Jayne?'

Popular Perks

'As I see it, our only hope is to provide a much better package of fringe benefits for young married women. I'd like you to look at this report from the *Daily Telegraph*,' she said. 'It shows the kinds of fringe benefits which 450 employers provide for office staff.'

Most Popular Perks
Proportion of employers providing benefits to office staff (%)

Sick and maternity leave	100
Pension scheme	96
Training in office skills	92
Life or accident insurance	86
Canteen or dining room	68
Medical insurance	64
Social club	51
Share option/profit sharing	37
Office outing	27
Flexible hours scheme	23
Assistance with transport	23
Marriage gratuities	12
Nursery facilities	9
Hairdressing allowance	9

Source: Daily Telegraph,
22 November 1988 (adapted)

'We don't come out too badly,' said Ken, glancing up from the report. 'We provide all the top five benefits. Perhaps we ought to think about medical insurance again.'

'I costed that out six months ago,' said John. 'It would be very expensive.'

'That's right,' said Jayne. 'I think we could get a more attractive and cheaper package for married women by providing some of the other benefits on the list.'

'Share options might be popular,' said John. 'What do you think, Jayne?'

Jayne smiled. 'I'd vote for a hairdressing allowance every time.'

'That wouldn't do me much good!' said John, who was completely bald.

ACTIVITIES

Questions

1 According to the case study, what are the main effects of the Queen's Award on a firm's public image?

2 Why is the rate of labour turnover important in all firms?

3 What are the main problems of J F Brown Ltd in recruiting and retaining office staff?

4 Describe the general importance of fringe benefits in recruiting labour.

5 What package of extra fringe benefits would you advise J F Brown Ltd to provide for its office staff. Explain your reasons in full.

Residential Home

David Holt had worked for many years as a personnel officer in the social services department of the local council. His wife, Di, was a nurse. Although they both liked their jobs, they didn't see much of a future in them. So they decided to take a chance and set up their own business instead. After weeks of discussion, they came to the conclusion that a residential home for old people was most likely to succeed.

Di's experience as a nurse would be very useful in looking after old people. David's contacts with the social services department would be valuable in obtaining residents; and his long experience as a personnel officer would be helpful in recruiting suitable staff.

Ideal Area

The area where they lived also seemed ideal. It was a quiet, leafy suburb, with a number of old Victorian houses with large gardens.

They planned to sell their own house, and buy a bigger one and convert it into a residential home. David had already had a chat with a friend in the council's planning department about planning permission. His friend thought it would be easy to obtain, as there was a social need and no residential home in the area. David and Di hoped that their bank manager would give them a loan to carry out the conversion. With the help of one of David's council colleagues, they made out a business plan.

Bank Loan

They were surprised and delighted when the bank manager agreed to give them a loan, subject to their obtaining planning permission and a suitable property.

With this encouragement, they decided to put their own house on the market. They had quite a large number of enquiries. Shortly before their house was sold, they had another piece of luck.

David heard that a Christian hostel in the area was going to be sold. It was ideal for conversion, as it had ten single rooms, a small self-contained flat on the first floor, and extensive gardens.

Before the hostel was put on the market, David made an offer which was immediately accepted as the Christian community was pleased that their hostel was going to be used as a residential home.

There was no trouble in obtaining planning permission, subject to the property being brought up to the current standards for residential homes. Six months later, it was opened as a residential home for ten people.

Immediate Success

The home was a success right from the start, with every room occupied from the first day. They had a mixture of Department of Social Security and private patients at average fees of £170 a week.

They ran the home with the help of eight part-time staff. It was much harder work than they imagined, particularly as many of the part-time staff were unreliable.

Nevertheless, at the end of five years, they had paid off the bank loan and were making a good profit, as their accounts showed.

Income and Expenditure Account

	£	£
Turnover		88,000
Business rates	5,400	
Wages	15,000	
Interest	1,700	
Food	10,500	
Repairs and insurance	4,280	
Heat and lighting	4,600	
Advertising	620	
Telephone and postage	900	
Miscellaneous	2,000	
Net profit	43,000	
	88,000	88,000

Balance Sheet at 31 December

	£	£		£	£
Capital account	240,500		Building and land	245,000	
Net profit	43,000		Fixtures and Furnishings	85,000	
	283,500			330,000	
Less drawings	10,000		Depreciation	33,000	
		273,500			297,000
Creditors		5,000	Debtors		500
Provision for tax		11,000	Bank and cash		2,000
Overdraft		10,000			
		299,500			299,500

Expansion Plans

David was ambitious to expand the home. He had obtained planning permission to build on five more single rooms in the large garden, at an estimated cost of £90,000. As the business had done so well, his bank manager was willing to give him a three-year loan, which they would pay off at £3,100 a month.

When the loan was paid off, David thought he would be able to sell the business for £500,000 to £600,000 and retire in luxury at the age of 53.

Di had a different view. As they had always led a very active life, she thought they were too young to retire entirely. However, she wanted to live in her own house again instead of a small flat, and to be freed from some of the day-to-day responsibilities of running the home.

She suggested that they should keep the home as it was and appoint a full-time manager at a salary of £12,000 a year to run it under their supervision. They could borrow money on the security of the home to buy a house in the neighbourhood, so that they would not be so closely involved in running the business.

ACTIVITIES

Questions

1 Why did David and Di think a residential home would succeed?

2 What items would they have included in their business plan?

3 Why was planning permission for a residential home granted?

4 What was the percentage net profit of the business?

5 If they expanded the home, what would be the new turnover if all the rooms were occupied at an average fee of £170 a week?

6 Assuming that the percentage net profit remains the same, what would be the new net profit per year?

7 Would it be feasible to pay off the bank loan? Show your workings.

8 Which plan is more sensible — David's or Di's? Explain your reasons.

Production Problems

The core business of Startwell Ltd is making an economy range of car batteries for tyre, battery and exhaust centres throughout the country.

The firm relies heavily on seasonal sales during the long hard months of winter when the short hours of daylight and the freezing winter mornings give car batteries a punishing time. However, the winter of 1988 was so mild that the sales figures for the year were much flatter than usual.

As a result the firm's turnover was reduced from £7,610,000 in 1987 to £6,375,000 in 1988. The mild weather continued in the early months of 1989 so that sales remained just as flat.

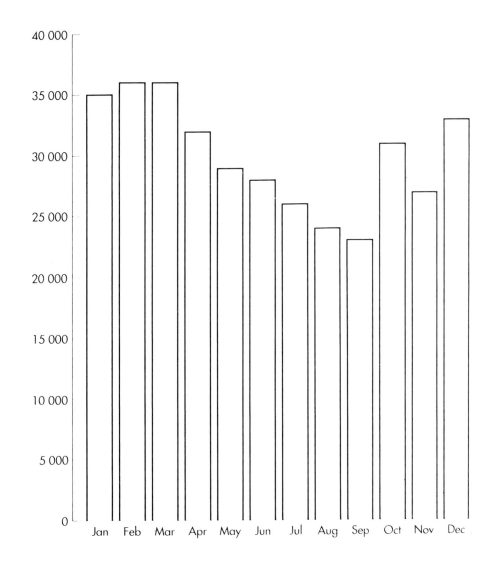

MONTHLY SALES

Another Problem

In addition to the mild weather, Startwell has another problem. Two years before, it bought a small car-battery manufacturing company at what seemed to be a bargain price, but it turned out to be anything but a bargain.

Shortly after the firm was taken over, there were a series of wildcat strikes, which disrupted production. A new Managing Director was appointed and output improved for a time.

In the last year, however, the unit costs of production have risen again, and there have been many breakdowns of machinery. (Sabotage was suspected, but it could not be proved.)

Only 20 per cent of the batteries are made at the smaller factory in Petersill. The rest are manufactured in the main factory at Hunshaw, which also makes emergency lighting equipment. The total output of car batteries in 1988 was 360,000.

Unit Costs

Although nothing could be done about the weather, the Managing Director decided that some action must be taken over the Petersill factory. He sent a memo to the Production Controller asking him for details of unit costs at the two factories.

Unit Costs of Production

	Hunshaw £	Petersill £
Direct costs		
Raw materials and freight charges	3.90	3.95
Labour costs	5.85	6.90
Indirect costs		
Factory costs	1.95	2.55
Total production costs	11.70	13.40
Overheads – including selling costs		
(allocated share of total)	1.30	0.30
	13.00	13.70

The Managing Director then called a meeting of top management to discuss the future of the Petersill plant.

Management Meeting

The Personnel Manager stated that he was currently trying to negotiate a productivity deal with the Petersill workers which would reduce labour costs there by 10 per cent, if it succeeded.

The Production Controller said he thought the productivity deal was unlikely to succeed, as the workforce was not highly motivated. Even if it did, labour costs would still be higher than they were at Hunshaw.

With the fall in sales, there was now spare capacity at Hunshaw, so that all the batteries could be made there with only a minimal increase in the labour force. It was an ideal time to close the Petersill plant.